**HARRAP'S SUPER-MINI**

# French
# Grammar

New York  Chicago  San Francisco  Lisbon  London  Madrid  Mexico City
Milan  New Delhi  San Juan  Seoul  Singapore  Sydney  Toronto

## The *McGraw·Hill* Companies

**Library of Congress Cataloging-in-Publication Data**

Harrap's super-mini French grammar / Harrap's.
        p.   cm. — (Harrap's super-mini's)
     ISBN 0-07-149234-8 (alk. paper)
      1. French language—Grammar.   I. Harrap (Firm)   II. Title: Super-mini
French grammar.
    PC2112.H35    2007
    448.2′421—dc22
                                           2007009031

1  2  3  4  5  6  7  8  9  10  11  12  13  14  15  16  17  18   TRA/TRA   0  9  8  7

ISBN-13: 978-0-07-149234-8
ISBN-10:   0-07-149234-8

### Titles in the *Harrap's Super-Mini* series:

| | | |
|---|---|---|
| French Grammar | Italian Grammar | Spanish Grammar |
| French Verbs | Italian Verbs | Spanish Verbs |
| French Vocabulary | Italian Vocabulary | Spanish Vocabulary |

This book is printed on acid-free paper.

# INTRODUCTION

This French grammar has been written to meet the new demands of language teaching in schools and colleges and is particularly suitable for exam revision. The essential rules of the French language have been set in terms that are as accessible as possible to all users. Where technical terms have been used, then full explanations of these terms have also been supplied. There is also a full glossary of grammatical terminology on pages 7-14. While literary aspects of the French language have not been ignored, the emphasis has been placed squarely on modern spoken French. This grammar, with its wealth of lively and typical illustrations of usage taken from the present-day language, is the ideal study tool for all levels – from the beginner who is starting to come to grips with the French language through to the advanced user who requires a comprehensive and readily accessible work of reference.

*Abbreviations used in the text:*

| | |
|---|---|
| *fem* | feminine |
| *masc* | masculine |
| *plur* | plural |
| *sing* | singular |

# CONTENTS

# CONTENTS

# 1. GLOSSARY OF GRAMMATICAL TERMS

## ADJECTIVE

An adjective provides supplementary information about a noun, describing what something is like, eg a *small* house, a *red* car, an *interesting* pastime.

## ADVERB

Adverbs are normally used with a verb to add extra information by indicating **how** the action is done (adverbs of manner), **when, where** or **with how much intensity** the action is done (adverbs of time, place and intensity), or **to what extent** the action is done (adverbs of quantity). Adverbs may also be used with an adjective or another adverb, eg a *very attractive girl, very well*.

## AGREEMENT

In French, words such as adjectives, articles and pronouns must agree in number and gender with the noun or pronoun to which they refer. This means that their spelling changes according to the **number** of the noun (singular or plural) and according to its **gender** (masculine or feminine).

## ANTECEDENT

The antecedent of a relative pronoun is the word or words to which the relative pronoun refers. The antecedent is usually found directly before the relative pronoun, eg in the sentence *I know **the man** who did this, the man* is the antecedent of *who*.

## APPOSITION

A word or a clause is said to be in apposition to another when it is placed directly after it without any joining word, eg *Mr Jones, **our bank manager**, rang today.*

# GLOSSARY

## ARTICLE

See DEFINITE ARTICLE, INDEFINITE ARTICLE and PARTITIVE ARTICLE.

## ASPIRATE H

If a word begins with an aspirate h in French, it means that there is no liaison between it and the word preceding it, eg in **les haricots** the **s** of **les** is not pronounced. Similarly, there is no contraction in spelling, eg **la haine** and not **l'haine**. See SILENT H.

## AUXILIARY

The French auxiliary verbs are **avoir** (*to have*) and **être** (*to be*). They are used to make up the first part of compound tenses, the second part being a past participle, eg *j'ai mangé, il est allé*.

## CARDINAL

Cardinal numbers are numbers such as *one, two, ten, fourteen*, as opposed to **ordinal** numbers, eg *first, second*.

## CLAUSE

A clause is a group of words which contains at least a subject and a verb: *he said* is a clause. A clause often contains more than this basic information, eg *he said this to her yesterday*. Sentences can be made up of several clauses, eg *he said/he'd call me/if he were free*. See SENTENCE.

## COMPARATIVE

The comparative forms of adjectives and adverbs allow two things, persons or actions to be compared. In English, *more … than, …er than, less … than* and *as … as* are used for comparison.

## COMPOUND

Compound tenses are verb tenses consisting of more than one element. In French, the compound tenses of a verb are formed by the **auxiliary** verb and the **past participle**: *j'ai visité, il est venu*.

## CONDITIONAL

This mood is used to describe what someone would do, or something that would happen if a condition were fulfilled, eg *I **would come** if I were well; the chair **would have broken** if he had sat on it.*

## CONJUGATION

The conjugation of a verb is the set of different forms taken in the particular tenses of that verb.

## CONJUNCTION

Conjunctions are used to link different clauses. They may be coordinating or subordinating. Coordinating conjunctions are words like *and, but, or*; subordinating conjunctions are words like *because, after, although*.

## DEFINITE ARTICLE

The definite article is *the* in English and *le, la* and *les* in French.

## DEMONSTRATIVE

Demonstrative adjectives such as *this, that, these* and pronouns such as *this one, that one* are used to point out a particular person or object.

## DIRECT OBJECT

A direct object is a noun or a pronoun which in English follows a verb without any linking preposition, eg *I met a **friend**.*

## ELISION

Elision consists in replacing the last letter of certain words (*le, la, je, me, te, se, de, que*) with an apostrophe before a word starting with a **vowel** or a **silent h**, eg *l'eau, l'homme, j'aime*.

## ENDING

The ending of a verb is determined by the **person** (1st/2nd/3rd) and **number** (singular/plural) of its subject. In French, most tenses have six different endings. See PERSON and NUMBER.

# GLOSSARY

## EXCLAMATION

An exclamation is a word or sentence used to express surprise or wonder, eg *what!, how!, how lucky!, what a nice day!*

## FEMININE

See GENDER.

## GENDER

The gender of a noun indicates whether the noun is **masculine** or **feminine** (all French nouns are either masculine or feminine).

## IDIOMATIC EXPRESSIONS

Idiomatic expressions (or idioms) are expressions which cannot normally be translated word for word. For example, *it's raining cats and dogs* is translated by *il pleut des cordes*.

## IMPERATIVE

This mood is used for giving orders, eg *eat!, don't go!*

## INDEFINITE

Indefinite pronouns and adjectives are words that do not refer to a definite person or object, eg *each, someone, every.*

## INDEFINITE ARTICLE

The indefinite article is *a* in English and *un, une* and *des* in French.

## INDICATIVE

The indicative is the normal form of a verb as in *I like, he came, we are trying.* It is opposed to the subjunctive, conditional and imperative.

## INDIRECT OBJECT

An indirect object is a pronoun or noun which follows a verb indirectly, with a linking preposition (usually **to**), eg *I spoke to **my friend/him**.*

## INFINITIVE

The infinitive is the basic form of the verb as found in dictionaries. Thus *to eat, to finish, to take* are infinitives. In French, the infinitive is recognizable by its ending (**-er**, **-ir** or **-re**, eg *manger, finir, prendre*).

## INTERROGATIVE

Interrogative words are used to ask a question. This may be a direct question (***when** will you arrive?*) or an indirect question (*I don't know **when** he'll arrive*). See QUESTION.

## MASCULINE

See GENDER.

## MOOD

This is the name given to the four main areas within which a verb is conjugated. See INDICATIVE, SUBJUNCTIVE, CONDITIONAL, IMPERATIVE.

## NOUN

A noun is a word or group of words which refers to a living creature, a thing, a place or an abstract idea, eg *postman, cat, shop, passport, life*.

## NUMBER

The number of a noun indicates whether the noun is **singular** or **plural**. A singular noun refers to one single person or thing, eg *boy, train* and a plural noun to more than one, eg *boys, trains*.

## ORDINAL

Ordinal numbers are *first, second, third, fourth* and all other numbers which end in **-th**. In French, all ordinal numbers, except for *premier* (first) and *second* (second), end in **-ième**.

## PARTITIVE ARTICLE

The partitive articles are *some* and *any* in English and *du, de la, de l'* and *des* (as in *du pain, de la confiture, de l'eau, des bananes*) in French.

# GLOSSARY

## PASSIVE

A verb is used in the passive when the subject of the verb does not perform the action but is subjected to it. The passive is formed with the verb **to be** and the past participle of the verb, eg *he was rewarded*.

## PAST PARTICIPLE

The past participle of a verb is the form which is used after **to have** in English, eg *I have* **eaten**, *I have* **said**, *you have* **tried**.

## PERSON

In any tense, there are three persons in the singular (1st: *I* ..., 2nd: *you* ..., 3rd: *he/she* ...), and three in the plural (1st: *we* ..., 2nd: *you* ..., 3rd: *they* ...). See also ENDING.

## PERSONAL PRONOUNS

Personal pronouns stand for a noun. They usually accompany a verb and can be either the subject (*I, you, he/she/it, we, they*) or the object of the verb (*me, you, him/her/it, us, them*).

## PLURAL

See NUMBER.

## POSSESSIVE

Possessive adjectives and pronouns are used to indicate possession or ownership. They are words like *my/mine, your/yours, our/ours*.

## PREPOSITION

Prepositions are words such as *with, in, to, at*. They are followed by a noun or a pronoun.

## PRESENT PARTICIPLE

The present participle is the verb form which ends in **-ing** in English and **-ant** in French.

## PRONOUN

This is a word which stands for a noun. The main categories of pronouns are:

- **Relative pronouns** (eg *who, which, that*)
- **Interrogative pronouns** (eg *who?, what?, which?*)
- **Demonstrative pronouns** (eg *this, that, these*)
- **Possessive pronouns** (eg *mine, yours, his*)
- **Personal pronouns** (eg *you, him, us*)
- **Reflexive pronouns** (eg *myself, himself*)
- **Indefinite pronouns** (eg *something, all*)

## QUESTION

There are two question forms: **direct** questions stand on their own and require a question mark at the end, eg *when will he come?*; **indirect** questions are introduced by a clause and require no question mark, eg *I wonder when he will come.*

## REFLEXIVE

Reflexive verbs 'reflect' the action back onto the subject, eg *I dressed myself.* They are always found with a reflexive pronoun and are much more common in French than in English.

## SENTENCE

A sentence is a group of words made up of one or more clauses (see CLAUSE) and which makes a complete grammatical structure. The end of a sentence is indicated by a punctuation mark (usually a full stop, a question mark or an exclamation mark).

## SILENT H

The term 'silent h' is actually misleading since an **h** is never pronounced in French. The point is that when a silent **h** occurs, any preceding vowel is not pronounced either. For example, the **h** in *j'habite* is silent (note the *j'*). The **h** in *je hurle*, however, is **aspirate**, and so there is no contraction in spelling.

# GLOSSARY

## SIMPLE TENSE

Simple tenses are tenses in which the verb consists of one word only, eg *j'habite, Maurice partira*.

## SINGULAR

See NUMBER.

## SUBJECT

The subject of a verb is the noun or pronoun which performs the action. In the sentences, *the train left early* and *she bought a record, the train* and *she* are the subjects.

## SUBJUNCTIVE

The subjunctive is a verb form which is rarely used in English, eg *if I were you, God save the Queen*, but common in French.

## SUPERLATIVE

The superlative is the form of an adjective or an adverb which, in English, is marked by *the most …, the …est* or *the least …*

## TENSE

Verbs are used in tenses, which tell us whether an action takes place in the present, the past or the future.

## VERB

A verb is a word which describes the performance of an action, eg *to sing, to work, to watch* or the existence of a state, eg *to be, to have, to hope*.

# 2. ARTICLES

## A. The Definite Article

### 1. Forms

In English, there is only one form of the definite article: **the**. In French, there are three forms, depending on the gender and number of the noun following the article:

- with a masculine singular noun: **le**
- with a feminine singular noun: **la**     } the
- with a plural noun (masc or fem): **les**

| MASC SING | FEM SING | PLURAL |
|---|---|---|
| **le chauffeur** | **la secrétaire** | **les étudiants** |
| the driver | the secretary | the students |
| **le salon** | **la cuisine** | **les chambres** |
| the living-room | the kitchen | the bedrooms |

*Note:* **le** and **la** both change to **l'** before a vowel or a silent **h**:

| | MASCULINE | FEMININE |
|---|---|---|
| BEFORE VOWEL | **l'avion** | **l'odeur** |
| | the plane | the smell |
| BEFORE SILENT H | **l'homme** | **l'hôtesse** |
| | the man | the hostess |

*Pronunciation:* the **s** of **les** is pronounced **z** when the noun following it begins with a vowel or a silent **h**.

### 2. Forms with the prepositions 'à' and 'de'

When the definite article is used with **à** or **de**, the following spelling changes take place:

a) with *à* (to, at)

| à + le | → | au |
|---|---|---|
| à + les | → | aux |

à + la and à + l' do not change

**au restaurant**
at/to the restaurant

**aux enfants**
to the children

**à la plage**
at/to the beach

**à l'aéroport**
at/to the airport

*Pronunciation:* the **x** of **aux** is pronounced **z** when the noun following it begins with a vowel or a silent **h**.

b) *with de (of, from)*

de + le       →       du

de + les      →       des

de + la and de + l' do not change

**du directeur**
of/from the manager

**des chômeurs**
of/from the unemployed

**de la région**
of/from the area

**de l'usine**
of/from the factory

*Pronunciation:* the **s** of **des** is pronounced **z** when the noun following it begins with a vowel or a silent **h**.

## 3. Use

As in English, the definite article is used when referring to a particular person or thing, or particular persons or things:

**les amis dont je t'ai parlé**
the friends I told you about

**le café est prêt**
the coffee is ready

However, the definite article is used far more frequently in French than in English. It is used in particular in the following cases where English uses no article:

a) *when the noun is used in a general sense*

i) to refer to all things of a kind:

**vous acceptez les chèques?**
do you take cheques?

**le sucre est mauvais pour les dents**
sugar is bad for the teeth

ii)  to refer to abstract things:

**le travail et les loisirs**
work and leisure

**la musique classique**
classical music

iii)  when stating likes and dislikes:

**j'aime la viande mais je préfère le poisson**
I like meat, but I prefer fish

**je déteste les tomates**
I hate tomatoes

**b)** *with geographical names*

i)  continents, countries and areas:

| | | |
|---|---|---|
| **le Canada**<br>Canada | **la France**<br>France | **l'Europe**<br>Europe |
| **la Bretagne**<br>Brittany | **l'Afrique**<br>Africa | **les États-Unis**<br>the United States |

*But:* the article **la** is omitted with the prepositions **en** and **de** when used with feminine country names:

**j'habite en France**
I live in France

**il vient d'Italie**
he comes from Italy

With masculine country names, the corresponding prepositions **à** and **de** follow the normal rules:

**j'habite au Portugal/aux États-Unis**
I live in Portugal/in the United States

**je viens du Japon/des Pays-Bas**
I come from Japan/the Netherlands

A very few country names do not require an article, eg **Panamá, Cuba, Taïwan, Singapour**.

ii)  mountains, lakes and rivers:

**le mont Everest**
Mount Everest

**le lac de Genève**
Lake Geneva

**c)** *with names of seasons*

| | |
|---|---|
| **l'automne** | autumn |
| **l'hiver** | winter |
| **le printemps** | spring |
| **l'été** | summer |

# ARTICLES

*But:*   **en automne/été/hiver**
in autumn/summer/winter

**au printemps**
in spring

**un jour d'été**
a summer's day

d) *with names of languages*

**j'apprends le français**
I'm learning French

*But:*   **ce film est en anglais**
this film is in English

e) *with parts of the body*

**j'ai les cheveux roux**
I've got red hair

**ouvrez la bouche**
open your mouth

**les mains en l'air!**
hands up!

**l'homme à la barbe noire**
the man with the black beard

f) *with names following an adjective*

**le petit Pierre**
little Pierre

**la pauvre Isabelle**
poor Isabelle

g) *with titles*

**le docteur Coste**
Doctor Coste

**le commandant Cousteau**
Captain Cousteau

h) *with days of the week to express regular occurrences*

**que fais-tu le samedi?**
what do you do on Saturdays?

**le docteur reçoit le lundi et le vendredi**
the doctor sees patients on Mondays and Fridays

i) *with names of subjects or leisure activities*

**les maths**
maths

**l'histoire et la géographie**
history and geography

**la natation, la lecture, le football**
swimming, reading, football

j) *in expressions of price, quantity etc*

**c'est combien le kilo/la douzaine/la bouteille?**
how much is it for a kilo/dozen/bottle?

# B. The Indefinite Article

## 1. Forms

In French, there are three forms of the indefinite article, depending on the number and gender of the noun it accompanies:

- with a masculine singular noun:    **un**    a
- with a feminine singular noun:    **une**    a
- with a plural noun (masc or fem):    **des**    some

*Note:* **des** is often not translated in English:

> **il y a des nuages dans le ciel**
> there are clouds in the sky

## 2. Use

a) On the whole, the French indefinite article is used in the same way as its English equivalent:

| **un homme** | **une femme** | **des hommes/ femmes** |
|---|---|---|
| a man | a woman | (some) men/ women |
| **un livre** | **une tasse** | **des livres/tasses** |
| a book | a cup | (some) books/cups |

b) However, the English indefinite article is not always translated in French:

i) when stating someone's profession or occupation:

> **mon père est architecte**
> my father is an architect

> **elle est médecin**
> she is a doctor

Note, however, that the article is used after **c'est, c'était** etc:

> **c'est un acteur célèbre**
> he's a famous actor

**ce sont des fraises**
these are strawberries

ii) with nouns in apposition:

**Madame Leclerc, employée de bureau**
Mrs Leclerc, an office worker

iii) after **quel** in exclamations:

**quel dommage!**
what a pity!

**quelle surprise!**
what a surprise!

c) In negative sentences, **de** (or **d'**) is used instead of **un, une, des**:

**je n'ai pas d'amis**
I don't have any friends

**je n'ai plus de voiture**
I don't have a car any more

d) In French (but not in English), the indefinite article is used with abstract nouns followed by an adjective:

**avec une patience remarquable**
with remarkable patience

**elle a fait des progrès étonnants**
she's made amazing progress

Note, however, that the article is not used when there is no adjective:

**avec plaisir**
with pleasure

**sans hésitation**
without hesitation

# C. The Partitive Article

## 1. Forms

There are three forms of the French partitive article, which corresponds to 'some'/'any' in English:

- □ with a masculine singular noun:  **du**
- □ with a feminine singular noun:  **de la**
- □ with plural nouns (masc or fem):  **des**

| **du vin** | **de la bière** | **des fruits** |
|---|---|---|
| some wine | some beer | some fruit |

Note that **de l'** is used in front of masculine or feminine singular nouns beginning with a vowel or a silent **h**:

| **de l'argent** | **de l'eau** |
|---|---|
| some money | some water |

**de l'helium**
some helium

## 2. Use

**a)** On the whole, the French partitive article is used as in English. However, English tends to omit the partitive article where French does not:

| **achète du pain** | **vous avez du beurre?** |
|---|---|
| buy (some) bread | do you have (any) butter? |

| **je voudrais de la viande** | **tu veux de la soupe?** |
|---|---|
| I'd like some meat | do you want (any) soup? |

| **tu dois manger des légumes** | **as-tu acheté des poires?** |
|---|---|
| you must eat (some) vegetables | did you buy any pears? |

**b)** The partitive article is replaced by **de** (or **d'**) in the following cases:

i) in negative expressions:

| **il n'y a plus de café** | **je n'ai pas de frères** |
|---|---|
| there isn't any coffee left | I don't have any brothers |

**nous n'avons plus d'argent**      **je n'ai pas d'enfants**
we don't have any money left      I don't have any children

Note, however, that when the clause is introduced by **c'est, il est** etc, the partitive article remains:

**ce n'est pas du cuir, c'est du plastique**
it's not leather, it's plastic

ii) after expressions of quantity (see also pp 232-4):

**il boit trop de café**      **il gagne assez d'argent**
he drinks too much coffee      he earns enough money

iii) after **avoir besoin de**:

**j'ai besoin d'argent**      **tu as besoin de timbres?**
I need (some) money      do you need (any) stamps?

iv) where an adjective is followed by a plural noun:

**de petites villes**      **d'énormes mensonges**
(some) small towns      outrageous lies

Note, however, that if the adjective comes after the noun, **des** does not change:

**des résultats encourageants**
encouraging results

## 2. Partitive or definite article?

When no article is used in English, it is not always clear which is the right article in French: **le/la/les** or **du/de la/des**.

If **some/any** can be inserted before the English noun, the French partitive article should be used. But if the noun is used in a general sense and inserting **some/any** in front of the English noun does not make sense, the definite article must be used:

did you buy fish? (*ie any fish*)
**tu as acheté *du* poisson?**

yes, I did; I like fish (*ie fish in general*)
**oui; j'aime *le* poisson**

# 3. NOUNS

A noun is a word or group of words which refers to a person, an animal, a thing, a place or an abstract idea.

## A. Gender

All French nouns are either masculine or feminine; there is no neuter as in English. Though *no absolute rule can be stated*, the gender can often be determined either by the meaning or the ending of the noun.

### 1. Masculine

**a)** *by meaning*

i)   words referring to men and male animals:

| **un homme** | **le boucher** | **le tigre** |
|---|---|---|
| a man | the butcher | the tiger |

ii)  names of common trees and shrubs:

| **le chêne** | **le sapin** | **le laurier** |
|---|---|---|
| the oak | the fir tree | the laurel |

iii) days, months, seasons:

| **lundi** | **mars** | **le printemps** |
|---|---|---|
| Monday | March | spring |

iv) languages:

| **le français** | **le polonais** | **le russe** |
|---|---|---|
| French | Polish | Russian |

v)  rivers and countries not ending in a silent **e**:

| **le Nil** | **le Portugal** | **le Danemark** |
|---|---|---|
| the Nile | Portugal | Denmark |

Note, however, that there are exceptions to this rule:

| **le Danube** | **le Rhône** | **le Mexique** |
|---|---|---|
| the Danube | the Rhone | Mexico |

**b)** *by ending*

| | |
|---|---|
| -acle | **le spectacle** (show)<br>*But:* **une débâcle** (shambles) |
| -age | **le fromage** (cheese)<br>*But:* **la cage** (cage), **une image** (picture),<br>**la nage** (swimming), **la page** (page), **la**<br>**plage** (beach), **la rage** (rage, rabies) |
| -é | **le marché** (market)<br>*But:* nouns ending in **-té** and **-tié** are usually<br>feminine (see p 27) |
| -eau | **le chapeau** (hat)<br>*But:* **l'eau** (water), **la peau** (skin) |
| -ège | **le piège** (trap), **le collège** (secondary school) |
| -ème | **le thème** (theme, topic)<br>*But:* **la crème** (cream) |
| -isme, -asme | **le communisme** (communism), **le tourisme**<br>(tourism), **l'enthousiasme** (enthusiasm) |
| -o | **le numéro** (the number)<br>*But:* **la dynamo** (dynamo) and most<br>abbreviated expressions: **une auto** (car),<br>**la météo** (weather forecast), **la photo**<br>(photograph), **la radio** (radio), **la sténo**<br>(shorthand), **la stéréo** (stereo) |

Nouns ending in a *consonant* are usually *masculine*.

*Notable exceptions* are:

i) most nouns ending in **-tion, -sion, -ation, -aison, -ison**

ii) most abstract nouns ending in **-eur** (see p 27)

iii) the following nouns ending in a consonant:

| | |
|---|---|
| **la clef** (key) | **la nef** (nave) |
| **la soif** (thirst) | **la faim** (hunger) |
| **la fin** (end) | **la façon** (manner) |

| | |
|---|---|
| **la leçon** (lesson) | **la boisson** (drink) |
| **la moisson** (harvest) | **la rançon** (ransom) |
| **la mer** (sea) | **la cuiller** (spoon) |
| **la chair** (flesh) | **la basse-cour** (farmyard) |
| **la cour** (yard) | **la tour** (tower) |
| **la brebis** (ewe) | **une fois** (once) |
| **la vis** (screw) | **la souris** (mouse) |
| **la part** (share) | **la plupart** (majority, most) |
| **la dent** (tooth) | **la dot** (dowry) |
| **la forêt** (forest) | **la jument** (mare) |
| **la mort** (death) | **la nuit** (night) |
| **la croix** (cross) | **la noix** (nut) |
| **la paix** (peace) | **la perdrix** (partridge) |
| **la toux** (cough) | **la voix** (voice) |

## 2. Feminine

**a)** *by meaning*

i) words referring to women and female animals:

| **la mère** | **la bonne** | **la génisse** |
|---|---|---|
| the mother | the maid | the heifer |

ii) names of rivers and countries ending with a silent **e**:

| **la Seine** | **la Russie** | **la Belgique** |
|---|---|---|
| the Seine | Russia | Belgium |

iii) saints' days and festivals:

| **la Toussaint** | **la Pentecôte** |
|---|---|
| All Saints' Day | Whitsun |

Note, however, that **Noël** (Christmas) is masculine except when used with the definite article: **à la Noël** (at Christmas)

**b)** *by ending*

| -ace | **la place** (square, seat) |
|---|---|
| | *But:* **un espace** (space) |
| -ade | **la salade** (salad) |
| | *But:* **le grade** (degree, rank), **le stade** (stadium) |
| -ance, -anse | **la puissance** (power), **la danse** (dancing) |
| -ée | **la soirée** (evening), **la journée** (day) |

| | |
|---|---|
| | *But:* **le musée** (museum), **le lycée** (secondary school) |
| -ence, -ense | **une évidence** (evidence), **la défense** (defence) |
| | *But:* **le silence** (silence) |
| -ère | **la lumière** (light) |
| | *But:* **le mystère** (mystery), **le caractère** (character) |
| -eur | **la peur** (fear) |
| | *But:* **le bonheur** (happiness), **le chœur** (choir), **le cœur** (heart), **un honneur** (honour), **le labeur** (toil), **le malheur** (misfortune) |
| -ie | **la pluie** (rain) |
| | *But:* **le génie** (genius), **un incendie** (fire), **le parapluie** (umbrella) |
| -ière | **la bière** (beer) |
| | *But:* **le cimetière** (cemetery) |
| -oire | **la gloire** (glory) |
| | *But:* **le laboratoire** (laboratory), **le pourboire** (tip) |
| -tion, -sion, -ation, -aison, -ison | |
| | **la fiction** (fiction), **la nation** (nation), **la raison** (reason), **la prison** (prison) |
| -té | **la bonté** (goodness) |
| | *But:* **le côté** (side), **le comté** (county), **le traité** (treaty), **le pâté** (pâté) |
| -tié | **la moitié** (half), **la pitié** (pity) |

Most nouns ending in a silent **e** following two consonants are feminine:

**la botte** (boot), **la couronne** (crown), **la terre** (earth), **la masse** (mass), **la lutte** (struggle)

*But:* **le verre** (glass), **le parterre** (flower-bed), **le tonnerre** (thunder), **un intervalle** (interval), **le carrosse** (carriage)

## 3. Difficulties

a) Some nouns may have either gender depending on the sex of the person to whom they refer:

| | |
|---|---|
| **un artiste** | **une artiste** |
| a (male) artist | a (female) artist |
| **le Russe** | **la Russe** |
| the Russian (man) | the Russian (woman) |

similarly:

| | |
|---|---|
| **un aide/une aide** | an assistant |
| **un camarade/une camarade** | a friend |
| **un domestique/une domestique** | a servant |
| **un enfant/une enfant** | a child |
| **un malade/une malade** | a patient |
| **un propriétaire/une propriétaire** | an owner |

b) Others have only one gender for both sexes:

| | | |
|---|---|---|
| **un ange** | **un amateur** | **un auteur** |
| an angel | an amateur | an author |
| **une connaissance** | **une dupe** | **un écrivain** |
| an acquaintance | a dupe | a writer |
| **une personne** | **le médecin** | **le peintre** |
| a person | the doctor | the painter |
| **la recrue** | **le sculpteur** | **la sentinelle** |
| the recruit | the sculptor (sculptress) | the sentry |
| **le témoin** | **la victime** | **la vedette** |
| the witness | the victim | the (film) star |

Note, however, that modern French tends to use feminine forms for many different functions. **La ministre**, **la juge** and **la professeur** can now be commonly found in the press, and new forms such as **une écrivaine** have also begun to appear.

c) The following nouns change meaning according to gender:

|  | MASCULINE | FEMININE |
|---|---|---|
| aide | male assistant | assistance, female assistant |
| crêpe | mourning band | pancake |
| critique | critic | criticism |
| faux | forgery | scythe |
| livre | book | pound |
| manche | handle | sleeve |
| manuvre | labourer | manoeuvre |
| mémoire | memorandum | memory |
| mode | method, way | fashion |
| mort | dead man | death |
| moule | mould | mussel |
| page | pageboy | page |
| pendule | pendulum | clock |
| physique | physique | physics |
| poêle | stove | frying pan |
| poste | post (*job*), set | post office |
| somme | nap | sum |
| tour | trick, tour | tower |
| trompette | trumpeter | trumpet |
| vapeur | steamer | steam |
| vase | vase | silt |
| voile | veil | sail |

d) A few words vary in gender according to their usage. The plural noun **gens** is regarded as feminine when it follows an adjective, and masculine when it precedes it:

**de bonnes gens**　　　　　　　**des gens ennuyeux**
good people　　　　　　　　　　boring people

**amour, délice** and **orgue** are masculine when used in the singular and feminine when used in the plural:

**un amour de jeunesse**　　　　**des amours malheureuses**
an old flame　　　　　　　　　　unhappy love affairs

**un délice inoubliable**　　　　**des délices infinies**
an unforgettable delight　　　　infinite delights

29

      **un orgue électrique**       **les grandes orgues**
      an electric organ       the great organ

e) *City names*

Some city names are traditionally feminine:

| **La Rochelle** | **La Haye** | **Alger la Blanche** |
|---|---|---|
| La Rochelle | The Hague | Algiers, the white city |

Others are masculine in everyday usage:

**le Paris des années 30**       **le Londres de mon souvenir**
Paris in the 30s       the London I remember

**le vieux Nice**       **Berlin fut totalement détruit**
old Nice       Berlin was completely
      destroyed

In literary French, however, city names are feminine:

**Caen fut prise après de terribles bombardements**
Caen was taken after a terrible bombardment

# B. The Formation Of Feminines

The feminine of nouns may be formed in the following ways:

**1.** By adding an **e** to the masculine form:

| | |
|---|---|
| **un ami** | **une amie** |
| a (male) friend | a (female) friend |
| **un Hollandais** | **une Hollandaise** |
| a Dutchman | a Dutch woman |

Note that nouns which end in **-e** in the masculine form do not change:

| | |
|---|---|
| **un élève** | **une élève** |
| a (male) pupil | a (female) pupil |

Note also that the addition of an **e** often entails an alteration of the masculine form:

i) nouns ending in **-t** and **-n** double the final consonant:

| | |
|---|---|
| **le chien** | **la chienne** (dog/bitch) |
| **le chat** | **la chatte** (cat) |

ii) nouns ending in **-er** add a grave accent to the **e** immediately preceding the **r**:

**un ouvrier**   **une ouvrière** (workman/female worker)

iii) nouns ending in **-eur** change into **-euse**:

**le vendeur**   **la vendeuse** (male/female shop assistant)

However, a few nouns ending in **-eur** change into **-eresse**:

**le pécheur**   **la pécheresse** (sinner)

iv) nouns ending in **-teur** change into **-teuse** or **-trice** according to the following guidelines:

if the stem of the word is also that of a present participle the feminine form ends in **-euse**:

**le chanteur**   **la chanteuse** (male/female singer)

if the stem is not that of a present participle, the feminine form ends in **-trice**:

**le lecteur**      **la lectrice** (male/female reader)

v) nouns ending in **-f** change into **-ve**:

**le veuf**      **la veuve** (widower/widow)

vi) nouns ending in **-x** change into **-se**:

**un époux**      **une épouse** (husband/wife)

vii) nouns ending in **-eau** change into **-elle**:

**le jumeau**      **la jumelle** (male/female twin)

**2.** By using a different word (as in English):

| | |
|---|---|
| **le beau-fils** | **la belle-fille** (son-/daughter-in-law) |
| **le beau-père** | **la belle-mère** (father-/mother-in-law) |
| **le bélier** | **la brebis** (ram/ewe) |
| **le bœuf** | **la vache** (ox/cow) |
| **le canard** | **la cane** (drake/duck) |
| **le cheval** | **la jument** (horse/mare) |
| **le cerf** | **la biche** (stag/hind) |
| **le coq** | **la poule** (cock/hen) |
| **le fils** | **la fille** (son/daughter) |
| **le frère** | **la sœur** (brother/sister) |
| **un homme** | **une femme** (man/woman) |
| **un jars** | **une oie** (gander/goose) |
| **le mâle** | **la femelle** (male/female) |
| **le neveu** | **la nièce** (nephew/niece) |
| **un oncle** | **une tante** (uncle/aunt) |
| **le parrain** | **la marraine** (godfather/godmother) |
| **le père** | **la mère** (father/mother) |
| **le porc** | **la truie** (pig/sow) |
| **le roi** | **la reine** (king/queen) |

**3.** By adding the word **femme** (or **femelle** for animals):

**une femme médecin** (doctor)
**un perroquet femelle** (female parrot)

## 4. Irregular feminine forms

| | |
|---|---|
| un abbé | **une abbesse** (abbot/abbess) |
| un âne | **une ânesse** (donkey) |
| le comte | **la comtesse** (count/countess) |
| le dieu | **la déesse** (god/goddess) |
| le duc | **la duchesse** (duke/duchess) |
| un Esquimau | **une Esquimaude** (Eskimo) |
| le fou | **la folle** (madman/mad woman) |
| un Grec | **une Grecque** (Greek) |
| un héros | **une héroïne** (hero/heroine) |
| un hôte | **une hôtesse** (host/hostess) |
| le maître | **la maîtresse** (master/mistress) |
| le prêtre | **la prêtresse** (priest/priestess) |
| le prince | **la princesse** (prince/princess) |
| le tigre | **la tigresse** (tiger/tigress) |
| le Turc | **la Turque** (Turk) |
| le vieux | **la vieille** (old man/old woman) |

## C. The Formation Of Plurals

**1.** Most nouns form their plural by adding **s** to the singular:

| | | |
|---|---|---|
| le vin | les vins | wine |
| un étudiant | des étudiants | student |

**2.** Nouns ending in **-s**, **-x** or **-z** remain unchanged:

| | | |
|---|---|---|
| le bras | les bras | arm |
| la voix | les voix | voice |
| le nez | les nez | nose |

**3.** Nouns ending in **-au**, **-eau** and **-eu** add **x** to the singular:

| | | |
|---|---|---|
| le tuyau | les tuyaux | drainpipe |
| le bateau | les bateaux | boat |
| le jeu | les jeux | game |
| *But:* le landau | les landaus | pram |
| le bleu | les bleus | bruise |
| le pneu | les pneus | tyre |

**4.** Nouns ending in **-al** change to **-aux**:

| | | |
|---|---|---|
| le journal | les journaux | newspaper |
| *But:* le bal | les bals | dance |
| le carnaval | les carnavals | carnival |
| le festival | les festivals | festival |

**5.** Nouns ending in **-ail** change to **-aux**:

| | | |
|---|---|---|
| le bail | les baux | lease |
| le travail | les travaux | work |
| le vitrail | les vitraux | stained-glass window |
| *But:* le détail | les détails | detail |
| l'épouvantail | les épouvantails | scarecrow |
| l'éventail | les éventails | fan |
| le rail | les rails | rail |

**6.** Nouns ending in **-ou**:

**a)** Seven nouns ending in **-ou** add **x** in the plural:

| | | |
|---|---|---|
| le bijou | les bijoux | jewel |
| le caillou | les cailloux | pebble |
| le chou | les choux | cabbage |
| le genou | les genoux | knee |
| le hibou | les hiboux | owl |
| le joujou | les joujoux | toy |
| le pou | les poux | louse |

**b)** Other nouns ending in **-ou** add **s**:

| | | |
|---|---|---|
| le clou | les clous | nail |

## 7. Plural of compound nouns:

Each noun ought to be checked individually in a dictionary:

| | | | |
|---|---|---|---|
| *eg* | le chou-fleur | les choux-fleurs | cauliflower |
| | le beau-père | les beaux-pères | father-in-law |
| *But:* | un essuie-glace | des essuie-glaces | windscreen wiper |
| | le tire-bouchon | les tire-bouchons | corkscrew |

## 8. Irregular plurals:

| | | |
|---|---|---|
| un œil | des yeux | eye |
| le ciel | les cieux | sky |
| Monsieur | Messieurs | Mr |
| Madame | Mesdames | Mrs |
| Mademoiselle | Mesdemoiselles | Miss |

## 9. Collective nouns:

**a)** Some nouns are singular in French but plural in English:

| | |
|---|---|
| le bétail | cattle |
| la recette | takings |
| la police | police |

la police *a* arrêté certains grévistes
the police *have* arrested some strikers

**b)** Others are plural in French but singular in English:

| | |
|---|---|
| **le nouvelles** | news |
| **les capitaux** | capital |
| **les cheveux** | hair |

**les nouvelles** *sont* **bonnes**
the news *is* good

## 10. Proper nouns:

**a)** Ordinary family names are invariable:

**j'ai rencontré les Leblanc**
I met the Leblancs

**b)** Historical names add **-s**:

| | | |
|---|---|---|
| **les Stuarts** | **les Bourbons** | **les Tudors** |
| the Stuarts | the Bourbons | the Tudors |

# 4. ADJECTIVES

Adjectives usually accompany a noun (or a pronoun) and provide extra information about what someone or something is like:

> **une *grande* ville**
> a *large* city

> **un passe-temps *intéressant***
> an *interesting* pastime

> **elle est *espagnole***
> she is *Spanish*

> **c'était *ennuyeux***
> it was *boring*

## A. Agreement Of Adjectives

In French, adjectives agree in number and gender with the noun or pronoun to which they refer. This means that French adjectives have four different forms which are determined by the noun they accompany:

> ❑ **masculine singular** (basic form, found in the dictionary)
> ❑ **feminine singular**
> ❑ **masculine plural**
> ❑ **feminine plural**

> **un passeport *vert***
> a green passport

> **une voiture *verte***
> a green car

> **des gants *verts***
> green gloves

> **des chaussettes *vertes***
> green socks

Note that if two singular words share the same adjective, the adjective will be in the plural:

> **un foulard et un bonnet *rouges***
> a red scarf and (a red) hat

If one of these words is feminine and the other masculine, the adjective will be in the masculine plural:

> **une robe et un manteau *noirs***
> a black dress and (a black) coat

## B. Feminine Forms Of Adjectives

### 1. General rule

Add the letter **e** to the masculine singular form:

| MASCULINE | FEMININE |
|---|---|
| grand | grande |
| amusant | amusante |
| anglais | anglaise |
| bronzé | bronzée |

| | |
|---|---|
| un livre amusant | une histoire amusante |
| an amusing book | an amusing story |
| | |
| il est bronzé | elle est bronzée |
| he is suntanned | she is suntanned |

### 2. Adjectives already ending in -e

These do not change:

| MASCULINE | FEMININE |
|---|---|
| rouge | rouge |
| jeune | jeune |
| malade | malade |

| | |
|---|---|
| mon père est malade | ma mère est malade |
| my father is ill | my mother is ill |

### 3. Others

The spelling of some adjectives changes when the **e** is added:

a) The following masculine endings generally double the final consonant before adding **e**:

| MASCULINE ENDING | FEMININE ENDING |
|---|---|
| -el | -elle |
| -eil | -eille |
| -en | -enne |
| -on | -onne |
| -as | -asse |
| -et | -ette |

| MASCULINE | | FEMININE |
|---|---|---|
| réel | (real) | réelle |
| cruel | (cruel) | cruelle |
| pareil | (similar) | pareille |
| ancien | (old) | ancienne |
| italien | (Italian) | italienne |
| bon | (good) | bonne |
| gras | (greasy) | grasse |
| bas | (low) | basse |
| muet | (dumb) | muette |
| net | (clear) | nette |

| | |
|---|---|
| **un problème actuel**<br>a topical problem | **la vie actuelle**<br>present-day life |
| **un bon conseil**<br>good advice | **c'est une bonne recette**<br>it's a good recipe |

Note, however, that the feminine ending of some common adjectives in **-et** is **-ète** instead of **-ette**:

| MASCULINE | | FEMININE |
|---|---|---|
| complet | (complete) | complète |
| incomplet | (incomplete) | incomplète |
| concret | (concrete) | concrète |
| discret | (discreet) | discrète |
| inquiet | (worried) | inquiète |
| secret | (secret) | secrète |

b)
| MASCULINE<br>IN **-er** | | FEMININE<br>IN **-ère** |
|---|---|---|
| cher | (dear) | chère |
| fier | (proud) | fière |
| dernier | (last) | dernière |

c)
| MASCULINE<br>IN **-x** | | FEMININE<br>IN **-se** |
|---|---|---|
| heureux | (happy) | heureuse |
| malheureux | (unhappy) | malheureuse |
| sérieux | (serious) | sérieuse |
| jaloux | (jealous) | jalouse |

| *But:* | **doux** | (soft) | **douce** |
| | **faux** | (false) | **fausse** |
| | **roux** | (red-haired) | **rousse** |
| | **vieux** | (old) | **vieille** |

d) | MASCULINE<br>IN **-eur** | | FEMININE<br>IN **-euse** |
|---|---|---|
| **menteur** | (lying) | **menteuse** |
| **trompeur** | (deceitful) | **trompeuse** |

This rule, however, applies only when the stem of the adjective is also the stem of a present participle (eg **mentant, trompant**). The following five adjectives simply add an **e** to the feminine, **-eur** becoming **-eure**:

| MASCULINE | | FEMININE |
|---|---|---|
| **extérieur** | (external) | **extérieure** |
| **intérieur** | (internal) | **intérieure** |
| **inférieur** | (inferior) | **inférieure** |
| **supérieur** | (superior) | **supérieure** |
| **meilleur** | (better) | **meilleure** |

The feminine ending of the remaining adjectives in **-teur** is **-trice**:

| MASCULINE | | FEMININE |
|---|---|---|
| **protecteur** | (protective) | **protectrice** |
| **destructeur** | (destructive) | **destructrice** |

e) | MASCULINE<br>IN **-f** | | FEMININE<br>IN **-ve** |
|---|---|---|
| **neuf** | (new) | **neuve** |
| **vif** | (lively) | **vive** |
| **naïf** | (naive) | **naïve** |
| **actif** | (active) | **active** |
| **passif** | (passive) | **passive** |
| **positif** | (positive) | **positive** |
| **bref** | (brief) | **brève** (note the **è**) |

**f)**

| MASCULINE<br>IN -c | | FEMININE<br>IN -che or -que |
|---|---|---|
| blanc | (white) | blanche |
| franc | (frank) | franche |
| sec | (dry) | **sèche** (note that the e changes to **è**) |
| public | (public) | publique |
| turc | (Turkish) | turque |
| grec | (Greek) | grecque (note the c) |

**g)** The following five common adjectives have an irregular feminine form and two forms for the masculine singular; the second masculine form, based on the feminine form, is used before words starting with a vowel or a silent **h**:

| MASCULINE | FEMININE | MASCULINE 2 |
|---|---|---|
| **beau**<br>(beautiful) | **belle** | **bel** |
| **nouveau**<br>(new) | **nouvelle** | **nouvel** |
| **vieux**<br>(old) | **vieille** | **vieil** |
| **fou**<br>(mad) | **folle** | **fol** |
| **mou**<br>(soft) | **molle** | **mol** |
| **un beau lac**<br>a beautiful lake | **une belle vue**<br>a beautiful view | **un bel enfant**<br>a beautiful child |
| **un nouveau disque**<br>a new record | **la nouvelle année**<br>the new year | **un nouvel ami**<br>a new friend |
| **un vieux tableau**<br>an old painting | **la vieille ville**<br>the old town | **un vieil homme**<br>an old man |

**h)** Other irregular feminines:

| MASCULINE | | FEMININE |
|---|---|---|
| **favori** | (favourite) | **favorite** |
| **gentil** | (nice) | **gentille** |
| **nul** | (no) | **nulle** |

41

## ADJECTIVES

| | | |
|---|---|---|
| frais | (fresh) | fraîche |
| malin | (shrewd) | maligne |
| sot | (foolish) | sotte |
| long | (long) | longue |
| aigu | (sharp) | aiguë |
| ambigu | (ambiguous) | ambiguë |
| chic | (elegant) | chic |
| châtain | (chestnut) | châtain |

## C. Plurals Of Adjectives

### 1. General rule

The masculine and feminine plural of adjectives is formed by adding an **s** to the singular form:

| | |
|---|---|
| **un vélo neuf**<br>a new bike | **des vélos neufs**<br>new bikes |
| **une belle fleur**<br>a beautiful flower | **de belles fleurs**<br>beautiful flowers |
| **le livre intéressant**<br>the interesting book | **les livres intéressants**<br>the interesting books |

### 2. Adjectives ending in -s or -x

If the masculine singular ends in **-s** or **-x**, the plural form does not take an **s**:

| | |
|---|---|
| **il est heureux**<br>he's happy | **ils sont heureux**<br>they are happy |
| **un touriste anglais**<br>an English tourist | **des touristes anglais**<br>English tourists |

### 3. Others

A few masculine plurals are irregular (the feminine plurals are all regular):

a)

| | SINGULAR<br>IN **-al** | | PLURAL<br>IN **-aux** |
|---|---|---|---|
| | **normal** | (normal) | **normaux** |
| | **brutal** | (brutal) | **brutaux** |
| | **loyal** | (loyal) | **loyaux** |
| *But:* | **fatal** | (fatal) | **fatals** |
| | **natal** | (native) | **natals** |
| | **naval** | (naval) | **navals** |

Note that the adjective **final** (final) has two masculine plural forms: **finals** and **finaux**.

**b)**

| SINGULAR IN -eau | | PLURAL IN -eaux |
|---|---|---|
| **beau** | (beautiful) | **beaux** |
| **nouveau** | (new) | **nouveaux** |

## D. Position Of Adjectives

**1.** Unlike English adjectives, French adjectives usually follow the noun:

**un métier intéressant**  **des parents modernes**
an interesting job   modern parents

Adjectives of colour and nationality always follow the noun:

**des chaussures rouges**  **le drapeau britannique**
red shoes   the British flag

**2.** However, the following common adjectives generally come before the noun:

| | |
|---|---|
| beau | beautiful |
| bon | good |
| court | short |
| gentil | nice |
| grand | big, tall |
| gros | fat |
| haut | high |
| jeune | young |
| joli | pretty |
| long | long |
| mauvais | bad |
| méchant | nasty, naughty |
| meilleur | better |
| moindre | lesser, least |
| petit | small |
| pire | worse |
| vieux | old |
| vilain | nasty, ugly |

**3.** Some adjectives have a different meaning according to their position:

| | BEFORE NOUN | AFTER NOUN |
|---|---|---|
| ancien | former | ancient |
| brave | good | brave |
| certain | some | sure |
| cher | dear | expensive |

# ADJECTIVES

|  | BEFORE NOUN | AFTER NOUN |
|---|---|---|
| **dernier** | last (*final*) | last (*latest*) |
| **grand** | great (*people only*) | big, tall |
| **même** | same | very |
| **pauvre** | poor (*pitiable*) | poor (*not rich*) |
| **propre** | own | clean |
| **seul** | single, only | alone, lonely |
| **simple** | mere | simple |
| **vrai** | real | true |

**mon ancien métier**
my former job

**un tableau ancien**
an old painting

**un brave type**
a nice fellow

**un homme brave**
a brave man

**un certain charme**
a certain charm

**un fait certain**
a definite fact

**chère Brigitte**
dear Brigitte

**un cadeau cher**
an expensive present

**la dernière séance**
the last performance

**le mois dernier**
last month

**une grande vedette**
a great star

**un homme assez grand**
a fairly tall man

**le même endroit**
the same place

**la vérité même**
the truth itself

**mon pauvre ami!**
my poor friend!

**des gens pauvres**
poor people

**mon propre frère**
my own brother

**une chambre propre**
a clean room

**mon seul espoir**
my only hope

**un homme seul**
a lonely man

**un simple employé**
an ordinary employee

**des goûts simples**
simple tastes

**un vrai casse-pieds**
a real bore

**une histoire vraie**
a true story

If a noun is accompanied by several adjectives, the same rules apply to each of them:

**le bon vieux temps**
the good old days

**un joli foulard rouge**
a pretty red scarf

# E. Comparative And Superlative Of Adjectives

Persons or things can be compared by using:

1. *the comparative form of the adjective:*

   more … than

   …er than

   less … than

   not as … as

   as … as

2. *the superlative form of the adjective:*

   the most …

   the …est

   the least …

## 1. The comparative

The French comparative is formed as follows:

| | | |
|---|---|---|
| **plus … (que)** | **plus long** | **plus cher** |
| more … (than) | longer | more expensive |
| …er (than) | | |
| **moins … (que)** | **moins long** | **moins récent** |
| less … (than) | less long | less recent |
| not as … (as) | | |
| **aussi … (que)** | **aussi bon** | **aussi important** |
| as … (as) | as good | as important |

**une plus grande maison**      **un village plus ancien**
a larger house                         an older village

**le football est-il plus populaire que le rugby?**
is football more popular than rugby?

**ces gants sont moins chauds que les autres**
these gloves are less warm than the other ones

**elle est beaucoup/bien moins patiente que lui**
she's far less patient than he is

le problème de la pollution est tout aussi grave
the pollution problem is just as serious

## 2. The superlative

a) *Formation*

le/la/les plus ...          the most ..., the ...est
le/la/les moins ...         the least ...

le plus grand pays          la plus grande ville
the largest country         the largest city

les plus grands acteurs     les plus grandes voitures
the greatest actors         the largest cars

b) *Word order*

i) The normal rules governing word order of adjectives apply. When a superlative adjective comes after the noun, the article is used twice, before the noun and before the adjective:

le plat le plus délicieux
the most delicious dish

l'histoire la plus passionnante
the most exciting story

ii) When a possessive adjective is used, there are two possible constructions, depending on the position of the adjective:

ma plus forte matière
my best subject

*or:*  mon besoin le plus urgent est de trouver un emploi
my most urgent need is to find a job

c) *'in' is normally translated by* **de***:*

la plus jolie maison du quartier/de la ville
the prettiest house in the area/town

le restaurant le plus cher de France
the most expensive restaurant in France

Note that verbs following the superlative usually take the subjunctive (see p 138).

### 3. Irregular comparatives and superlatives

| ADJECTIVE | COMPARATIVE | SUPERLATIVE |
| --- | --- | --- |
| **bon** | **meilleur** | **le meilleur** |
| good | better | best |
| **mauvais** | **pire** | **le pire** |
| | **plus mauvais** | **le plus mauvais** |
| bad | worse | the worst |
| **petit** | **moindre** | **le moindre** |
| | **plus petit** | **le plus petit** |
| small | smaller, lesser | the smallest, the least |

Note that **pire** and **le pire** are, strictly speaking, the correct comparative and superlative forms of **mauvais**. **Plus mauvais** and **le plus mauvais** can also be found in everyday French, however, with a slight difference in meaning: **pire** and **le pire** express the absolute (ie one cannot conceive of a worse example of …) while **plus mauvais** and **le plus mauvais** indicate a comparison of a lesser degree:

> **il n'y a pas de pire professeur que lui**
> he is the worst teacher of all

> **c'est la pire chose qui pouvait lui arriver**
> it's the worst thing that could happen to him

> **ma note est plus mauvaise que la tienne**
> my mark is worse than yours

> **c'est le plus mauvais élève de la classe**
> he's the worst pupil in the class

Note, too, that **moindre** usually means 'less in importance', and **plus petit** 'less in size':

> **le moindre de mes soucis**
> the least of my worries

> **elle est plus petite que moi**
> she is smaller than I (am)

## F. Adjectives Of Nationality

**1.** French, unlike English, does not use capital letters for adjectives of nationality. Only nouns indicating nationality are written with a capital letter in French:

**une voiture anglaise**
an English car

**une Anglaise**
an English woman

**2.** An adjective of nationality in English is sometimes best translated by a genitive construction in French:

**l'ambassade de France**
the French embassy

**l'équipe de France de rugby**
the French rugby team

**l'équipe de Nantes**
the Nantes team

**l'équipe de Glasgow**
the Glasgow *or* Glaswegian team

**le championnat de France**
the French league

**le Coupe de France de football**
the French football cup

**la Grand Prix du Brésil**
the Brazilian Grand Prix

**la terre de France**
French soil

**la couronne de France**
the French crown, the crown of France

**les côtes de France**
the French coastline

**une grammaire de l'anglais**
an English grammar

# 5. ADVERBS

Adverbs are normally used with a verb to express:

| | | ADVERBS OF |
|---|---|---|
| how | | manner |
| when | | time |
| where | an action is done | place |
| with how much intensity | | intensity |
| to what extent | | quantity |

## A. Adverbs Of Manner

These are usually formed by adding **-ment** to the adjective (like **-ly** in English):

**1.** If the adjective ends in a consonant, **-ment** is added to its feminine form:

| ADJECTIVE (masc, fem) | ADVERB |
|---|---|
| **doux, douce** (soft) | **doucement** (softly) |
| **franc, franche** (frank) | **franchement** (frankly) |
| **final, finale** (final) | **finalement** (finally) |

**2.** If the adjective ends in a vowel, **-ment** is added to its masculine form:

| ADJECTIVE | ADVERB |
|---|---|
| **absolu** (absolute) | **absolument** (absolutely) |
| **désespéré** (desperate) | **désespérément** (desperately) |
| **vrai** (true) | **vraiment** (truly) |
| **simple** (simple) | **simplement** (simply) |

*But:*

| | |
|---|---|
| **gai** (cheerful) | **gaiement** *or* **gaîment** (cheerfully) |
| **nouveau** (new) | **nouvellement** (newly) |
| **fou** (mad) | **follement** (madly) |

**3.** Many adverbs have irregular forms:

**a)** Some change the **e** of the feminine form of the adjective to **é** before adding **-ment**:

| ADJECTIVE | ADVERB |
|---|---|
| **commun** (common) | **communément** (commonly) |
| **précis** (precise) | **précisément** (precisely) |
| **profond** (deep) | **profondément** (deeply) |
| **énorme** (enormous) | **énormément** (enormously) |
| **aveugle** (blind) | **aveuglément** (blindly) |

**b)** Adjectives which end in **-ent** and **-ant** change to **-emment** and **-amment**. Note that both endings are pronounced like **amant**:

| ADJECTIVE | ADVERB |
|---|---|
| **prudent** (careful) | **prudemment** (carefully) |
| **évident** (obvious) | **évidemment** (obviously) |
| **brillant** (brilliant) | **brillamment** (brilliantly) |
| *But:* **lent** (slow) | **lentement** (slowly) |

**4.** Some adverbs are completely irregular, including some of the most commonly used ones:

| ADJECTIVE | ADVERB |
|---|---|
| **bon** (good) | **bien** (well) |
| **bref** (brief) | **brièvement** (briefly) |
| **gentil** (kind) | **gentiment** (kindly) |
| **mauvais** (bad) | **mal** (badly) |
| **meilleur** (better) | **mieux** (better) |

**5.** Some adjectives are also used as adverbs in certain set expressions:

| | |
|---|---|
| **parler bas/haut** or **fort** | to speak softly/loudly |
| **coûter/payer cher** | to cost/pay a lot |
| **s'arrêter net** | to stop short |
| **couper court** | to cut short |
| **voir clair** | to see clearly |
| **marcher droit** | to walk straight |
| **travailler dur** | to work hard |

| | |
|---|---|
| chanter faux/juste | to sing off key/in tune |
| sentir mauvais/bon | to smell bad/good |
| refuser net | to refuse point blank |

**6.** After verbs relating to saying something or looking at something in French an adverbial phrase is often preferred to an adverb:

**'tu m'écriras?' dit-il** *d'une voix triste*
'will you write to me?' he said *sadly*

**elle nous a regardés** *d'un air dédaigneux*
she looked at us *disdainfully*

**7.** English adverbs may be expressed in French by a preposition followed by a noun:

| | |
|---|---|
| sans soin | carelessly |
| avec fierté | proudly |
| avec amour | lovingly |

## B. Adverbs Of Time

These are not usually formed from adjectives. The commonest ones are the following:

| | |
|---|---|
| alors | then |
| après | afterwards |
| aujourd'hui | today |
| aussitôt | at once |
| bientôt | soon |
| d'abord | first |
| déjà | already |
| demain | tomorrow |
| encore | still, again |
| pas encore | not yet |
| enfin | at last, finally |
| hier | yesterday |
| parfois | sometimes |
| rarement | seldom |
| souvent | often |
| tard | late |
| tôt | early |
| toujours | always |
| tout de suite | immediately |

c'est déjà Noël!
it's Christmas already!

tu as déjà essayé?
have you tried before?

il mange encore!
he's still eating!

elle n'est pas encore arrivée
she hasn't arrived yet

## C. Adverbs Of Place

Like adverbs of time, these are not usually formed from adjectives. The commonest ones are the following:

| | |
|---|---|
| ailleurs | somewhere else, elsewhere |
| ici | here |
| là | there |
| loin | far away |
| dessus | on top, on it |
| au-dessus | over, above |
| dessous | underneath |
| au-dessous | below |
| dedans | inside |
| dehors | outside |
| devant | in front, ahead |
| derrière | behind |
| partout | everywhere |

**ne restez pas dehors!**
don't stay outside!

**mon nom est marqué dessus**
my name is written on it

**qu'est-ce qu'il y a dedans?**
what's inside?

**passez devant**
go in front

## D. Adverbs Of Intensity And Quantity

These may be used with a verb, an adjective or another adverb. The commonest ones are the following:

| | |
|---|---|
| à peine | hardly |
| assez | enough, quite |
| autant | as much/many |
| beaucoup | a lot, much/many |
| combien | how much/many |
| comme | how |
| moins | less |
| plus | more |
| presque | nearly |
| peu | little |
| seulement | only |
| si | so |
| tant | so much/many |
| tellement | so much/many |
| très | very |
| trop | too, too much/many |
| un peu | a little |

**vous avez assez bu!**
you've had enough to drink!

**il ne fait pas assez chaud**
it's not warm enough

**nous avons beaucoup ri**
we laughed a lot

**comme c'est amusant!**
how funny!

**je vais un peu mieux**
I'm feeling a little better

**c'est si fatigant!**
it's so tiring!

**elle parle trop**
she talks too much

**il est très timide**
he's very shy

Note that all of these adverbs, except **à peine, comme, presque, si, très** and **seulement**, may be followed by **de** and a noun to express a quantity (see pp 232-3).

## E. Position Of Adverbs

**1.** Adverbs usually follow verbs:

> **je vais rarement au théâtre**
> I seldom go to the theatre

> **comme vous conduisez prudemment**
> you do drive carefully!

**2.** With compound tenses, shorter adverbs usually come between the auxiliary and the past participle:

> **j'ai enfin terminé**
> I have finished at last

> **nous y sommes souvent allés**
> we've often gone there

> **il me l'a déjà dit**
> he's already told me

> **elle avait beaucoup souffert**
> she had suffered a lot

**3.** Adverbs of place and many adverbs of time, however, follow the past participle:

> **je l'ai rencontré hier**
> I met him yesterday

> **elle avait cherché partout**
> she had looked everywhere

> **mettez-le dehors**
> put it outside

> **tu t'es couché tard?**
> did you go to bed late?

**4.** Adverbs usually come before adjectives or other adverbs, as in English:

> **très rarement**
> very seldom

> **trop vite**
> too quickly

> **elle est vraiment belle**
> she is really beautiful

## F. Comparative And Superlative Of Adverbs

**1.** The comparative and superlative of adverbs are formed in the same way as those of adjectives:

| ADVERB | COMPARATIVE | SUPERLATIVE |
|---|---|---|
| **souvent**<br>often | **plus souvent (que)**<br>more often (than) | **le plus souvent**<br>(the) most often |
| | **moins souvent (que)**<br>less often (than)<br>not as often (as) | **le moins souvent**<br>(the) least often |
| | **aussi souvent (que)**<br>as often (as) | |

Note that the superlative of the adverb always takes the masculine singular article **le**:

**je le vois plus souvent qu'avant**
I see him more often than I used to

**il conduit moins prudemment que moi**
he drives less carefully than I do
he doesn't drive as carefully as I do

**c'est lui qui conduit le moins prudemment**
he's the one who drives the least carefully

**je sais cuisiner aussi bien que toi!**
I can cook as well as you!

*Note:*

a) **as … as possible** is translated either by **aussi … que possible** or by **le plus …possible**:

as far as possible        **aussi loin que possible**
                               **le plus loin possible**

b) after a negative, **aussi** is often replaced by **si**:

**pas si vite!**
not so fast!

c) In French, the idea of **not so, not as** is often expressed by **moins** (less):

> **parle moins fort!**
> don't talk so loud!

## 2. Irregular comparatives and superlatives

| ADVERB | COMPARATIVE | SUPERLATIVE |
|---|---|---|
| **beaucoup** much, a lot | **plus** more | **le plus** (the) most |
| **bien** well | **mieux** better | **le mieux** (the) best |
| **mal** badly | **pis** or **plus mal** worse | **le pis** or **le plus mal** (the) worst |
| **peu** little | **moins** less | **le moins** (the) least |

> **il est mieux payé que moi**
> he is better paid than me

> **c'est lui le mieux payé**
> he's the best paid

*Note:*

a) **mieux/le mieux** must not be confused with **meilleur/ le meilleur** which are adjectives, used in front of a noun.

> **elle chante mieux que toi**
> she sings better than you (do)

> **c'est elle qui chante le mieux**
> she sings best

> **elle est meilleure chanteuse que toi**
> she is a better singer than you

> **c'est la meilleure chanteuse**
> she is the best singer

**b) pis/le pis** are only found in certain set expressions or in literary French:

> **tant pis**
> too bad
>
> **de mal en pis**
> from bad to worse
>
> **il n'y a rien de pis que cela**
> there is nothing worse than that
>
> **on en dit pris que pendre**
> nobody has a good word to say about it

# 6. PRONOUNS AND CORRESPONDING ADJECTIVES

## A. Demonstratives

### 1. Demonstrative adjectives

#### a) *CE*

**ce** is often used to point out a particular person or thing, or persons or things. It is followed by the noun to which it refers and agrees in number and gender with that noun:

- with a masculine singular noun: **ce (cet)** this/that
- with a feminine singular noun: **cette** this/that
- with a plural noun (masc or fem): **ces** these/those

**ce roman m'a beaucoup plu**
I really liked this novel

**il a neigé ce matin**
it snowed this morning

**cette chanson m'énerve**
that song gets on my nerves

**cette fois, c'est fini!**
this time, it's over!

**tu trouves que ces lunettes me vont bien?**
do you think these glasses suit me?

**cet** is used instead of **ce** in front of a masculine singular word that begins with a vowel or a silent **h**:

**cet été**
this summer

**cet hôtel**
that hotel

#### b) *-CI* and *-LÀ*

French does not have separate words to distinguish between 'this' and 'that'. However, when a particular emphasis is being placed on a person or object, or when a contrast is being made between persons or objects, **-ci** and **-là** are added to the noun:

**-ci** translates the idea of this/these
**-là** translates the idea of that/those

**je suis très occupé ces jours-ci**
I'm very busy these days

**que faisiez-vous ce soir-là?**
what were you doing that evening?

**tu préfères cette robe-ci ou cette robe-là?**
do you prefer this dress or that dress?

## 2. Demonstrative pronouns

Demonstrative pronouns are used instead of a noun with **ce/cette/ces**. They are:

> celui, celle, ceux, celles
> ce
> ceci, cela, ça

### a) *CELUI*

**celui** agrees in number and gender with the noun it refers to. It has four different forms:

|  | MASCULINE | FEMININE |
|---|---|---|
| SINGULAR | celui | celle |
| PLURAL | ceux | celles |

**celui**, **celle**, **ceux** and **celles** cannot be used on their own. They are used:

❑ with **-ci** or **-là**, for emphasis or for contrast:

| celui-ci | celle-ci | this (one) |
|---|---|---|
| celui-là | celle-là | that (one) |
| ceux-ci | celles-ci | these (ones) |
| ceux-là | celles-là | those (ones) |

**j'aime bien ce maillot mais celui-là est moins cher**
I like this swimsuit, but that one is cheaper

**je voudrais ces fleurs – lesquelles? celles-ci ou celles-là?**
I'd like these flowers – which ones? these or those?

❑ with **de** + noun, to express possession:

**je préfère mon ordinateur à celui de Jean-Claude**
I prefer my computer to Jean-Claude's

**range ta chambre plutôt que celle de ta sœur**
tidy your own bedroom rather than your sister's

**mes parents sont moins sévères que ceux de Nicole**
my parents aren't as strict as Nicole's

**les douches municipales sont mieux que celles du camping**
the public showers are better than those at the campsite

❑ with the relative pronouns **qui, que, dont** to introduce a relative clause (for use of these relative pronouns, see pp 93-9).

| | |
|---|---|
| celui/celle/ceux/celles qui | the one(s) who/which |
| celui/celle/ceux/celles que | the one(s) whom/which |
| celui/celle/ceux/celles dont | the one(s) of which/whose |

**lequel est ton père? celui qui a une moustache?**
which one is your father? the one with the moustache?

**regarde cette voiture! celle qui est garée au coin**
look at that car! the one which is parked at the corner

**deux filles, celles qu'il avait rencontrées la veille**
two girls, the ones he had met the day before

**voilà mon copain, celui dont je t'ai parlé l'autre jour**
here's my friend, the one I told you about the other day

## b) CE

**ce** (meaning 'it' or 'that') is normally used with the verb **être**:

| | | |
|---|---|---|
| c'est | ce serait | c'était |
| it's/that's | it/that would be | it/that was |

Note that **ce** changes to **c'** before an **e** or an **é**.

❑ with a noun or pronoun, **ce** is used to identify people or things, or to emphasize them; it is translated in a variety of ways:

**qu'est-ce que c'est? – c'est mon billet d'avion**
what's that? – it's my plane ticket

**qui est-ce? – c'est moi**
who is it? – it's me

**ce doit être lui**
that must be him

**c'est un artiste bien connu**
he's a well-known artist

**c'était une bonne idée**
it was a good idea

**ce sont mes amis**
they're my friends

**c'est la dernière fois!**
it's the last time!

**c'est elle qui l'a fait**
she's the one who did it

**c'est celui que j'ai vu**
he's the one I saw

**ce sont des gens
sympathiques**
they're nice people

**ce ne sont pas mes
chaussures**
those aren't my shoes

□ before an adjective, **ce** is used to refer to an idea, an event or a fact which has already been mentioned; it does not refer to any specific noun:

**c'était formidable**
it was great

**ce serait amusant**
it would be funny

**oui, c'est vrai**
yes, that's true

**c'est sûr?**
is that definite?

**ce n'est pas grave**
it doesn't matter *or* it's not serious

**c'est bon à entendre**
that's good to hear

**c'est exact!**
that's right!

**c'est rare qu'il pleuve en juin**
it doesn't often rain in June

Note that the translation of **it** is an area of some difficulty for students of French, as it is sometimes translated by **ce** and sometimes by **il/elle**; see pp 258-9 for further information.

c) *CECI, CELA, ÇA*

**ceci** (this), **cela** (that) and **ça** (that) are used to refer to an idea, an event, a fact or an object. They never refer to a particular noun already mentioned.

**non, je n'aime pas ça!**
no, I don't like that!

**ah, bon? cela m'étonne**
really? that surprises me

**ça, c'est un acteur!**
that's what I call an actor!

**souvenez-vous de ceci**
remember this

**ça m'est égal**
I don't mind

**cela ne vous regarde pas**
that's none of your business

**buvez ceci, ça vous fera du bien**
drink this, it'll do you good

**ça alors!**
well, really!

**cela s'appelle comment, en anglais?**
what do you call this in English?

Note that **ceci** is not very common in French; **cela** and **ça** are often used to translate 'this' as well as 'that'; **ça** is used far more frequently than **cela** in spoken French.

# B. Indefinite Adjectives And Pronouns

## 1. Indefinite adjectives

They are:

| MASCULINE | FEMININE | |
|---|---|---|
| autre(s) | autre(s) | other |
| certain(s) | certaine(s) | certain |
| chaque | chaque | each, every |
| même(s) | même(s) | same |
| plusieurs | plusieurs | several |
| quelque(s) | quelque(s) | some |
| tel(s) | telle(s) | such |
| tout (tous) | toute(s) | all, every |

Note that, when used as indefinite adjectives, all the above adjectives are placed before the nouns to which they refer. **Certain** and **même** can be found after the noun but they will then have a different meaning (see pp 45-6).

### a) *CHAQUE and PLUSIEURS*

**chaque** (each) is always singular, **plusieurs** (several) always plural; the feminine form is the same as the masculine form:

| | |
|---|---|
| **j'y vais chaque jour** | **chaque personne** |
| I go there every day | each person |
| **plusieurs années** | **il a plusieurs amis** |
| several years | he's got several friends |

### b) *AUTRE, MÊME and QUELQUE*

**autre** (other), **même** (same) and **quelque** (some) agree in number with the noun that follows; the feminine is the same as the masculine:

| | |
|---|---|
| **je voudrais un autre café** | **d'autres couleurs** |
| I'd like another coffee | other colours |
| **la même taille** | **les mêmes touristes** |
| the same size | the same tourists |

quelque temps après
some time later

à quelques kilomètres
a few kilometres away

### c) *CERTAIN, TEL* and *TOUT*

**certain** (certain, some), **tel** (such) and **tout** (all) agree in number and gender with the noun; they have four different forms:

**un certain charme**
a certain charm

**une certaine dame**
a certain lady

**à certains moments**
at (certain) times

**certaines personnes**
some people

**un tel homme**
such a man

**une telle aventure**
such an adventure

**de tels avantages**
such advantages

**de telles difficultés**
such difficulties

**quoi! tu as mangé tout le fromage et tous les fruits?**
what! you've eaten all the cheese and all the fruit?

**toute la journée**
all day long

**toutes mes matières**
all my subjects

*Note:*

i) **tel**: the position of the article **un/une** with **tel** is not the same as in English: **un tel homme** = such a man.

ii) **tel** cannot qualify another adjective; when it is used as an adverb, 'such' is translated by **si** or **tellement**:

**c'était un si bon repas/un repas tellement bon!**
it was such a good meal!

iii) **tous les/toutes les** are often translated by 'every':

**tous les jours**
every day

**toutes les places**
all seats, every seat

## 2. Indefinite pronouns

a) These are:

| MASCULINE | FEMININE | |
|---|---|---|
| aucun | aucune | none, not any |
| autre(s) | autre(s) | another one, other ones |
| certains | certaine(s) | certain, some |
| chacun | chacune | each one, every one, |
| on | | everyone, one, someone, you, they, people, we |
| personne | | nobody |
| plusieurs | plusieurs | several (ones) |
| quelque chose | | something, anything |
| quelqu'un | | someone |
| quelques-uns | quelques-unes | some, a few |
| rien | | nothing |
| tout (tous) | toute(s) | everything, every one, all |

**pas celui-là, l'autre**
not that one, the other one

**où sont les autres?**
where are the others?

**certains disent que …**
some say that …

**personne n'est venu**
no one came

**qui est là? – personne**
who's there? – nobody

**qu'as-tu? – rien**
what's wrong? – nothing

**plusieurs d'entre eux**
several of them

**chacun pour soi!**
every man for himself!

**il manque quelque chose?**
is anything missing?

**dis quelque chose!**
say something!

**quelqu'un l'a averti**
someone warned him

**il y a quelqu'un?**
is anyone in?

**j'ai tout oublié**
I've forgotten everything

**c'est tout, merci**
that's all, thanks

**elles sont toutes arrivées**
they've all arrived

**allons-y tous ensemble**
let's all go together

**b)** *Points to note*

i) **aucun(e)**, **personne** and **rien**: these can be used on their own, but they are more often used with a verb and the negative word **ne** (see negative expressions, pp 245-8):

**personne n'habite ici**
no one lives here

**il n'y a rien à manger**
there's nothing to eat

ii) **aucun(e)**, **un(e) autre**, **d'autres**, **certain(e)s**, **plusieurs** and **quelques-un(e)s**: when these pronouns are used as direct objects, the pronoun **en** must be used before the verb:

**je n'en ai lu aucun**
I haven't read any (of them)

**donne-m'en une autre**
give me another one

**j'en ai vu d'autres qui étaient moins chers**
I saw other ones which were cheaper

**j'en connais certains**
I know some of them

**il y en a plusieurs**
there are several

**tu m'en donnes quelques-uns?**
will you give me a few?

**achètes-en quelques-unes**
buy a few

iii) **personne, quelque chose, rien, plusieurs**: when these are followed by an adjective, the preposition **de** (or **d'**) must be used in front of the adjective:

**il n'y a personne de libre**
there's no one available

**quelque chose de mieux**
something better

**il y en avait plusieurs de cassés**
several of them were broken

**rien de grave**
nothing serious

iv) **autre** is commonly used in the following expressions:

**quelqu'un d'autre**
someone else

**quelque chose d'autre**
something else

**rien d'autre**
nothing else

## c) *ON*

This pronoun is used in a variety of ways in French. It can mean:

i) *one/you/they/people* in a general sense:

**en France, on roule à droite**
in France, they drive on the right

**on ne sait jamais**
you/one never know(s)

**on ne doit pas mentir**
you shouldn't lie

ii) *someone* (an undefined person)

In this sense, **on** is often translated by the passive (see p 161):

**on me l'a déjà dit**
someone's already told me
I've already been told

**on vous l'apportera**
someone will bring it to you
it will be brought to you

iii) *we*

In spoken French, **on** is frequently used instead of **nous**; although it refers to a plural subject, it is followed by the third person singular:

**qu'est-ce qu'on fait?**
what shall we do?

**fais vite, on t'attend!**
hurry up, we're waiting for you!

Note that in compound tenses with the auxiliary **être**, the agreement of the past participle with **on** is optional:

**on est allé au cinéma**
**on est allés au cinéma**
we went to the cinema

**on est rentré en taxi**
**on est rentrées en taxi**
we went home by taxi

## C. Interrogative And Exclamatory Adjectives And Pronouns

### 1. The interrogative adjective QUEL?

a) *Forms*

**quel** (which, what) agrees in number and gender with the noun it refers to. It has four forms:

- with a masculine singular noun: **quel?**
- with a feminine singular noun: **quelle?**
- with a masculine plural noun: **quels?**
- with a feminine plural noun: **quelles?**

b) *Direct questions:*

**quel est votre passe-temps favori?**
what's your favourite pastime?

**quelle heure est-il?**
what time is it?

**quels jours as-tu de libres?**
which days have you got free?

**quelles affaires comptes-tu prendre avec toi?**
what/which things do you intend to take with you?

c) *Indirect questions:*

**je ne sais pas quel CD choisir**
I don't know which CD to choose

**il se demande quelle veste lui va le mieux**
he's wondering which jacket suits him best

### 2. The exclamatory adjective QUEL!

**quel!** has the same forms as the interrogative adjective **quel?**:

**quel dommage!**
what a pity!

**quelle belle maison!**
what a beautiful house!

**quels imbéciles!**
what idiots!

**quelles jolies chaussures!**
what lovely shoes!

### 3. Interrogative pronouns

These are:

| | |
|---|---|
| **lequel/laquelle/** | which (one(s))? |
| **lesquels/lesquelles?** | |
| **qui?** | who?/whom? |
| **que?** | what? |
| **quoi?** | what? |
| **ce qui** | what |
| **ce que** | what |

**ce qui** and **ce que** are used only in indirect questions; all other interrogative pronouns can be used both in direct and indirect questions.

a) *LEQUEL?*

i) forms

**lequel** (which?, which one?) agrees in gender and in number with the noun it stands for:

- ◻ with a masculine singular noun: **lequel?** which (one)?
- ◻ with a feminine singular noun: **laquelle?** which (one)?
- ◻ with a masculine plural noun: **lesquels?** which (ones)?
- ◻ with a feminine plural noun: **lesquelles?** which (ones)?

After the prepositions **à** and **de**, the following changes occur:

| | | |
|---|---|---|
| à + lequel? | → | auquel? |
| à + lesquels? | → | auxquels? |
| à + lesquelles? | → | auxquelles? |
| de + lequel? | → | duquel? |
| de + lesquels? | → | desquels? |
| de + lesquelles? | → | desquelles? |

Note that **à/de + laquelle?** do not contract.

ii) direct questions:

**je cherche un hôtel; lequel recommandez-vous?**
I'm looking for a hotel; which one do you recommend?

**nous avons plusieurs couleurs; vous préférez laquelle?**
we have several colours; which one do you prefer?

**lesquels de ces livres sont à toi?**
which of these books are yours?

**je voudrais essayer ces chaussures – lesquelles?**
I would like to try these shoes on – which ones?

iii) indirect questions:

**demande-lui lequel de ces ordinateurs est le moins cher**
ask him/her which (one) of these computers is the cheapest

**c'est dans une de ces rues mais je ne sais plus laquelle**
it's in one of these streets, but I can't remember which one

## b) *QUI?*

**qui** (who?, whom?) is used to refer to people; it can be both subject and object and can be used after a preposition:

| | |
|---|---|
| **qui t'a accompagné?** | **qui as-tu appelé?** |
| who came/went with you? | who did you call? |
| **tu y vas avec qui?** | **c'est pour qui?** |
| who are you going with? | who is it for? |
| **pour qui vous prenez-vous?** | **à qui l'as-tu donné?** |
| who do you think you are? | who did you give it to? |

Note that **qui** does **not** contract to **qu'** before a vowel or a silent **h**:

**qui est-ce qu'elle attend?**
who is she waiting for?

**qui?** can be replaced by **qui est-ce qui?** (subject) or **qui est-ce que?** (object) in direct questions:

| | |
|---|---|
| **qui est-ce qui veut du café?** | **qui est-ce que tu as vu?** |
| who wants coffee? | who did you see? |

**avec qui est-ce que tu sors ce soir?**
who are you going out with tonight?

Note, however, that **qui** cannot be replaced by **qui est-ce qui** or **qui est-ce que** in indirect questions:

**j'aimerais savoir qui vous a dit ça**
I'd like to know who told you that

**elle se demandait de qui étaient les fleurs**
she was wondering who the flowers were from

For more details on the use of **qui/que** as relative pronouns, see pp 93-9.

### c) QUE?

**que** (what?) is used to refer to things. It is only used in direct questions, is always a direct object and cannot be used after prepositions:

**que désirez-vous?**          **qu'a-t-il dit?**
what do you wish?             what did he say?

**que?** is rather formal and is usually replaced by **qu'est-ce qui?** or **qu'est-ce que?** in spoken French.

Note that **que** becomes **qu'** before a vowel or a silent **h**.

### d) QU'EST-CE QUI?

**qu'est-ce qui?** (what?) is used as the subject of a verb; it cannot refer to a person:

**qu'est-ce qui t'est arrivé?**
what happened to you?

**qu'est-ce qui la fait rire?**
what makes her laugh?

### e) QU'EST-CE QUE?

**qu'est-ce que?** (what?) replaces **que?** as the object of a verb; it becomes **qu'est-ce qu'** before a vowel or a silent **h**:

**qu'est-ce que tu aimes lire?**
what do you like reading?

**qu'est-ce qu'il va faire pendant les vacances?**
what's he going to do during the holidays?

## f) *QUOI?*

**quoi?** (what?) refers to things; it is used:

i) instead of **que** or **qu'est-ce que** after a preposition:

**à quoi penses-tu?**        **dans quoi l'as-tu mis?**
what are you thinking about?    what did you put it in?

ii) in indirect questions:

**demandez-lui de quoi il a besoin**
ask him what he needs

**je ne sais pas à quoi ça sert**
I don't know what it's for

## g) *CE QUI, CE QUE*

**ce qui** and **ce que** (what) are only used in indirect questions; they replace **qu'est-ce qui** and **(qu'est-ce) que**.

They are used in the same way as the relative pronouns **ce qui** and **ce que** (see pp 97-9).

i) **ce qui** is used as the subject of the verb in the indirect question (**ce qui** is the subject of **s'est passé** in the following example):

**nous ne saurons jamais ce qui s'est passé**
we'll never know what happened

ii) **ce que** (**ce qu'** before a vowel or a silent **h**) is used as the object of the verb in the indirect question (**ce que** is the object of **il faisait** in the following example):

**je n'ai pas remarqué ce qu'il faisait**
I didn't notice what he was doing

# D. Personal Pronouns

There are four categories of personal pronouns:

- subject pronouns
- object pronouns
- disjunctive pronouns
- reflexive pronouns

For reflexive pronouns, see pp 118-9.

## 1. Subject pronouns

| PERSON | SINGULAR | | PLURAL | |
|--------|----------|--|--------|--|
| 1st | je (j') | I | nous | we |
| 2nd | tu | you | vous | you |
| 3rd | il | he, it | ils | they |
| | elle | she, it | elles | they |
| | on | one, we, they | | |

*Note:*

**a)** **je** changes to **j'** before a vowel or a silent **h**:

**j'ai honte**
I'm ashamed

**j'adore les frites**
I love chips

**j'habite en Écosse**
I live in Scotland

**b)** **tu** and **vous**

**vous** can be plural or singular; it is used when speaking to more than one person (plural), or to a stranger or an older person (singular):

**vous venez, les gars?**
are you coming, guys?

**pourriez-vous m'indiquer la gare?**
could you show me the way to the station?

**tu** is used when speaking to a friend, a relative, a younger person, or someone else you know well:

**tu viens, Marc?**
are you coming, Marc?

**c)** **il/ils, elle/elles** may refer to people, animals or things, and must be of the same gender as the noun they replace:

**ton stylo?** *il* **est là**
your pen? there *it* is

**ta montre?** *elle* **est là**
your watch? there *it* is

**tes gants?** *ils* **sont là**
your gloves? there *they* are

**tes lunettes?** *elles* **sont là**
your glasses? there *they* are

When referring to several nouns of different genders, French uses the masculine plural **ils**:

**j'ai trouvé dans mon sac** *un* **stylo et** *une* **montre.** *Ils* **ne m'appartiennent pas**
I found a pen and a watch in my bag. *They* don't belong to me

**d) on:** see p 71.

## 2. Object pronouns

There are three types of object pronouns:

□ direct object pronouns
□ indirect object pronouns
□ the pronouns **en** and **y**

**a)** *Forms*

| | PERSON | DIRECT | INDIRECT |
|---|---|---|---|
| SING | 1st | **me (m')** me | **me (m')** (to) me |
| | 2nd | **te (t')** you | **te (t')** (to) you |
| | 3rd | **le (l')** him, it | **lui** (to) him |
| | | **la (l')** her, it | **lui** (to) her |
| PLUR | 1st | **nous** us | **nous** (to) us |
| | 2nd | **vous** you | **vous** (to) you |
| | 3rd | **les** them | **leur** (to) them |

*Note:*

i) **me**, **te**, **le** and **la** change to **m'**, **t'** and **l'** before a vowel or a silent **h**:

**il m'énerve!**
he gets on my nerves!

**je m'habituerai à lui**
I'll get used to him

ii) **te** and **vous**: the same distinction should be made as between the subject pronouns **tu** and **vous** (see p 77).

iii) **le** is sometimes used in an impersonal sense to refer to a fact, a statement or an idea which has already been expressed; it is usually not translated in English:

**j'irai aux États-Unis un jour; en tout cas je *l*'espère**
I'll go to the States one day; I hope so anyway

**elle a eu un bébé – je *le* sais, elle me *l*'a dit**
she's had a baby – I know, she told me

iv) when used as an indirect object pronoun, **lui** can be masculine or feminine:

**pose-lui la question**
ask him/her the question

**j'ai décidé de lui offrir un cadeau**
I've decided to give him/her a present

v) when they are used with imperatives, **moi** and **toi** are used instead of **me** and **te**, except when **en** follows:

**écris-*moi* bientôt**
write to me soon

**donne *m*'en**
give me some

**b)** *Position*

In French, object pronouns come immediately before the verb they refer to. With a compound tense, they come before the auxiliary:

**on *t*'attendra ici**
we'll wait for you here

**je *l*'ai rencontrée en ville**
I met her in town

Note that when there are two verbs, the pronoun comes immediately before the verb to which it refers:

**j'aimerais lui demander**
I'd like to ask him/her

**tu l'as entendu chanter?**
have you heard him sing?

In positive commands (the affirmative imperative) the pronoun follows the verb and is joined to it by a hyphen:

**regarde-*les*!**　　　　　　　　**parle-*lui*!**
look at them!　　　　　　　　　speak to him/her!

**dis-*nous* ce qui s'est passé**
tell us what happened

c) *Direct pronouns and indirect pronouns*

i) Direct object pronouns replace a noun which directly follows the verb. They answer the question 'who(m)?' or 'what?'

WHO(M) did you see?　　　　　　I saw *my friend*; I saw *him*
**qui as-tu vu?**　　　　　　　　**j'ai vu *mon ami*; je *l'*ai vu**

**tu *me* connais**　　　　　　　**j'aime *le* voir danser**
you know *me*　　　　　　　　　I like to see *him* dance

**je *les* ai trouvés**　　　　　　**ne *nous* ennuie pas!**
I found *them*　　　　　　　　　don't bother *us*!

ii) Indirect object pronouns replace a noun which follows the verb with a linking preposition (usually **à**, to whom?). They answer the question 'who to?'

WHO did you speak to?　　　　　I spoke *to Marc*; I spoke *to him*
**à qui as-tu parlé?**　　　　　　**j'ai parlé *à Marc*; je *lui* ai**
　　　　　　　　　　　　　　　　**parlé**

**elle *lui* a menti**　　　　　　　**je *te* donne ce CD**
she lied *to him/her*　　　　　　I'm giving this CD *to you*

**je ne *leur* parle plus**
I'm not talking *to them* any more

iii) **le/la/les** or **lui/leur**?

Direct pronouns differ from indirect pronouns only in the 3rd person and great care must be taken to use the correct one:

□ English indirect object pronouns often look like direct objects; this becomes obvious when the object is placed at the end of the clause, after a linking preposition:

I showed him your photo　　=　　I showed your photo to him
　　　　　　　　　　　　　　　　**je *lui* ai montré ta photo**

This is particularly the case with the following verbs:

| | | | |
|---|---|---|---|
| **acheter** | to buy | **offrir** | to offer, to give |
| **donner** | to give | **prêter** | to lend |
| **montrer** | to show | **vendre** | to sell |

**je *lui* ai acheté un livre**
I bought him/her a book
= I bought a book *for him/her*

**ne *leur* prête pas mes affaires**
don't lend them my things
= don't lend my things *to them*

▫ Some verbs take a direct object in English and an indirect object in French (see p 204):

**je ne *lui* ai rien dit**
I didn't tell *him/her* anything

**tu *lui* ressembles**
you look like *him/her*

**je *leur* demanderai**
I'll ask *them*

**téléphone-*leur***
phone *them*

▫ Some verbs take a direct object in French and an indirect object in English (see p 203):

**je *l'*attends**
I'm waiting *for him/her*

**écoutez-*les*!**
listen *to them*!

**d)** *Order of object pronouns*

When several object pronouns are used together, they come in the following order:

i) Before the verb:

| 1 | me | te | | nous | vous |
|---|----|----|----|------|------|
| 2 | | le | la | | les |
| 3 | | | lui | leur | |

**il *me l'*a donné**
he gave it to me

**ne *la leur* vends pas**
don't sell it to them

**je vais *vous les* envoyer**
I'll send them to you

**je *le lui* ai acheté**
I bought it for him/her

ii) After the verb:

With a positive command (the affirmative imperative), the order is as follows:

| 1 | | le | la | | les | |
|---|---|---|---|---|---|---|
| 2 | moi (m') | toi (t') | | nous | | vous |
| 3 | | | lui | leur | | |

**apporte-*les-moi*!**
bring them to me!

**dites-*le-lui*!**
tell him/her!

**prête-*la-nous*!**
lend it to us!

**rends-*la-leur*!**
give it back to them!

### 3. The pronoun EN

a) *Use*

**en** is used instead of **de** + noun. Since **de** has a variety of meanings, **en** can be used in a number of ways:

i) It means 'of it/them', but also 'with it/them', 'about it/them', 'from it/there', 'out of it/there':

**tu es sûr *du prix*? – j'*en* suis sûr**
are you sure of the price? – I'm sure *of it*

**je suis content *de ce cadeau*; j'*en* suis content**
I'm pleased with this present; I'm pleased *with it*

**elle est folle *des animaux*; elle *en* est folle**
she's crazy about animals; she's crazy *about them*

**il est descendu *du train*; il *en* est descendu**
he got off the train; he got *off* it

**il revient *de Paris*; il *en* revient**
he's coming back from Paris; he's coming back *from there*

ii) Verbal constructions

Particular care should be taken with verbs and expressions which are followed by **de** + noun. Since **de** is not always translated in the same way, **en** may have a number of meanings:

**il a envie *de ce livre*; il *en* a envie**
he wants this book; he wants *it*

**je te remercie *de ton aide*; je t'*en* remercie**
thank you for your help; thank you *for it*

**tu as besoin *de ces papiers*? tu *en* as besoin?**
do you need these papers? do you need *them*?

**elle a peur *des chiens*; elle *en* a peur**
she's afraid of dogs; she's afraid *of them*

**tu te souviens *de ce film*? tu t'*en* souviens?**
do you remember this film? do you remember *it*?

iii) 'some'/'any'

**en** replaces the partitive article (**du, de la, des**) + noun; it means 'some'/'any':

**tu veux *du café*? – non, je n'*en* veux pas**
do you want (any) coffee? – no, I don't want *any*

**j'achète *des fruits*? – non, j'*en* ai chez moi**
shall I buy (some) fruit? – no, I've got *some* at home

**il y a *de la place*? – *en* voilà là-bas**
is there any room? – there's some over there

iv) Expressions of quantity

**en** must be used with expressions of quantity not followed by a noun. It replaces **de** + noun and means 'of it/them', but is seldom translated in English:

**tu as pris assez *d'argent*? tu *en* as pris assez?**
did you take enough money? did you take enough?

**vous avez *combien de frères*? – j'*en* ai deux**
how many brothers do you have? – I've got two

**j'ai fini *mes cigarettes*; je vais *en* acheter un paquet**
I've finished my cigarettes; I'm going to buy a packet

b) *Position*

Like object pronouns, **en** comes immediately before the verb, except with positive commands (the affirmative imperative), where it comes after the verb and is linked to it by a hyphen:

**j'en veux un kilo**
I want a kilo (of it/them)

**j'en ai marre!**
I'm fed up (with it)!

**prends-en assez!**
take enough (of it/them)!

**laisses-en aux autres!**
leave some for the others!

# PRONOUNS

When used in conjunction with other object pronouns, it always comes last:

**ne *m'en* parlez pas!**
don't tell me about it!

**je *vous* en donnerai**
I'll give you some

**prête-*lui*-en!**
lend him/her some!

**gardez-*nous*-en!**
keep some for us!

## 4. The pronoun Y

a) *Use*

**y** is used instead of **à** + noun, but never refers to a person. It is used:

i) As the indirect object of a verb. Since the preposition **à** is translated in a variety of ways in English, **y** may have various meanings (it, of it/them, about it/them etc):

**tu joues *au tennis*? – non, j'*y* joue rarement**
do you play tennis? – no, I seldom play (*it*)

**je pense *à mon pays natal*; j'*y* pense souvent**
I'm thinking *about* my home country; I often think *about it*

**il s'intéresse *à la photo*; il s'*y* intéresse**
he's interested in photography; he's interested *in it*

ii) To mean 'there':

**j'ai passé deux jours *à Londres*; j'*y* ai passé deux jours**
I spent two days in London; I spent two days there

**il est allé *en Grèce*; il *y* est allé**
he went to Greece; he went there

Note that **y** must always be used with the verb **aller** (to go) when the place is not mentioned in the clause. It is often not translated in English:

**comment vas-tu *à l'école*? – j'*y* vais en bus**
how do you get to school? – I go (there) by bus

**allons-*y*!**
let's go!

**on *y* va demain**
we're going (there) tomorrow

iii) To replace the prepositions **en, dans, sur** + noun; **y** then means 'there', 'in it/them', 'on it/them':

**je voudrais vivre** *en France*; **je voudrais y vivre**
I'd like to live in France; I'd like to live *there*

**je les ai mis** *dans ma poche*; **je les y ai mis**
I put them in my pocket; I put them *there*

*sur la table*? **non, je ne l'y vois pas**
on the table? no, I don't see it *there*

### b) *Position*

Like other object pronouns, **y** comes immediately before the verb, except with a positive command (the affirmative imperative), where it must follow the verb:

**j'y réfléchirai**
I'll think about it

**il s'y est habitué**
he got used to it

**pensez-*y*!**
think about it!

**n'y allez pas!**
don't go!

When used with other object pronouns, **y** comes last:

**il va** *nous* **y rencontrer**
he'll meet us there

**je** *l'y* **ai vu hier**
I saw him there yesterday

## 5. Disjunctive pronouns

### a) *Forms*

| PERSON | SINGULAR | PLURAL |
|---|---|---|
| 1st | **moi** | **nous** |
| | me | us |
| 2nd | **toi** | **vous** |
| | you | you |
| 3rd (masculine) | **lui** | **eux** |
| | him | them |
| (feminine) | **elle** | **elles** |
| | her | them |
| (impersonal) | **soi** | |
| | oneself | |

# PRONOUNS

*Note:*

i) **toi/vous**: the same difference should be made as between **tu** and **vous** (see p 77).

ii) **soi** is used in an impersonal, general sense to refer to indefinite pronouns and adjectives (**on, chacun, tout le monde, personne, chaque** etc); it is mainly found in set phrases, such as:

> **chacun pour soi**
> every man for himself

> **cela va de soi**
> that goes without saying

b) *Use*

Disjunctive pronouns, also called emphatic pronouns, are used instead of object pronouns when referring to persons in the following cases:

i) In answer to a question, alone or in a phrase without a verb:

> **qui est là? – moi**
> who's there? – me

> **j'ai aimé ce film; et toi?**
> I liked that film; did you?

> **qui préfères-tu, lui ou elle? – elle, bien sûr**
> who do you prefer, him or her? – her, of course

ii) After **c'est/ce sont, c'était/c'étaient** etc:

> **ouvrez, c'est moi!**
> open up, it's me!

> **non, ce n'était pas lui**
> no, it wasn't him

iii) After a preposition:

> **vous allez chez lui?**
> are you going to his place?

> **tu y vas avec elle?**
> are you going with her?

> **regarde devant toi!**
> look in front of you!

> **oh, c'est pour moi?**
> oh, is that for me?

iv) With verbal constructions. Special care should be taken when the verb is followed by a preposition:

> **tu peux compter sur moi**
> you can count on me

> **quoi! tu as peur de lui?**
> what! you're afraid of him?

il m'a parlé de toi
*he told me about you*

je pense souvent à vous
*I often think about you*

Note that emphatic pronouns are only used when referring to people. In other cases **y** or **en** must be used.

v) For emphasis, particularly when two pronouns are contrasted. The unstressed subject pronoun is usually included:

**vous, vous m'énervez!**
*you get on my nerves!*

**lui, il joue bien; elle, non**
*he plays well; she doesn't*

**moi, je n'aime pas l'hiver**
*I don't like winter*

**eux, ils sont partis**
*they've left*

vi) In the case of multiple subjects (two pronouns or one pronoun and one noun):

**lui et son frère sont dans l'équipe**
he and his brother are in the team

**ma famille et moi allons très bien**
my family and I are very well

vii) As the second element of a comparison:

**il est plus sympa que toi**
he is nicer than you

**elle chante mieux que lui**
she sings better than he does

viii) Before a relative pronoun:

**c'est lui que j'aime**
he's the one I love

**c'est toi qui l'as dit**
you're the one who said it

**lui qui n'aime pas le vin blanc en a bu six verres**
he who doesn't like white wine had six glasses

ix) With **-même(s)** (-self, -selves), **aussi** (too), **seul** (alone):

**faites-le vous-mêmes**
do it yourselves

**j'irai moi-même**
I'll go myself

**lui aussi est parti**
he too went away

**elle seule le sait**
she alone knows

x) To replace a possessive pronoun (see p 91-2):

**c'est le mien; il est à moi**
it's mine; it belongs to me

**cette valise n'est pas à lui?**
doesn't that suitcase belong to him?

# E. Possessive Adjectives And Pronouns

## 1. Possessive adjectives

a) *Forms*

Possessive adjectives always come before their related noun. Like other adjectives, they agree in gender and number with the noun; the masculine and feminine plural forms are identical:

| SINGULAR | | PLURAL | |
|----------|----------|----------|----------|
| MASC | FEM | (MASC AND FEM) | |
| mon | ma | mes | my |
| ton | ta | tes | your |
| son | sa | ses | his/her/its/one's |
| notre | notre | nos | our |
| votre | votre | vos | your |
| leur | leur | leurs | their |

**j'ai mis mon argent et mes affaires dans mon sac**
I've put my money and my things in my bag

**comment va ton frère? et ta sœur? et tes parents?**
how's your brother? and your sister? and your parents?

**notre rue est assez calme**      **ce sont vos amis**
our street is fairly quiet           they're your friends

Note that **mon/ton/son** are used instead of **ma/ta/sa** when the next word starts with a vowel or silent **h**:

**mon ancienne maison**      **ton amie Christine**
my old house                       your friend Christine

**son haleine sentait l'alcool**
his/her breath smelled of alcohol

b) *Use*

i) The possessive adjective is repeated before each noun and agrees in number and gender with it:

**mon père et ma mère sont sortis**
my mother and father have gone out

### ii) son/sa/ses

**son**, **sa** and **ses** can all mean 'his', 'her' or 'its'. In French, the form of the adjective is determined by the gender and number of the noun that follows, and not by the possessor:

**il m'a prêté sa mobylette et son casque**
he lent me his moped and his helmet

**elle s'entend bien avec sa mère mais pas avec son père**
she gets on well with her mother, but not with her father

**elle vit pour son travail; lui pour ses enfants**
she lives for her job; he lives for his children

### iii) ton/ta/tes and votre/vos

The two sets of words for 'your', **ton/ta/tes** and **votre/vos**, correspond to the two different forms of **tu** and **vous**; they must not be used together with the same person:

**tu as parlé à ton patron?**
have you spoken to your boss?

**Monsieur, vous oubliez votre parapluie!**
excuse me, sir, you've forgotten your umbrella!

iv) In French, the possessive adjective is replaced by the definite article (**le/la/les**) with the following:

□ parts of the body:

**il s'est essuyé les mains**          **elle a haussé les épaules**
he wiped his hands                     she shrugged (her shoulders)

□ descriptive phrases at the end of a clause, where English adds 'with':

**il marchait lentement, les mains dans les poches**
he was walking slowly, with his hands in his pockets

**elle l'a regardé partir, les larmes aux yeux**
she watched him leave with tears in her eyes

## 2. Possessive pronouns

| SINGULAR | | PLURAL | |
|----------|----|--------|----|
| MASC | FEM | (MASC AND FEM) | |
| le mien | la mienne | les mien(ne)s | mine |
| le tien | la tienne | les tien(ne)s | yours |
| le sien | la sienne | les sien(ne)s | his/hers/its |
| le nôtre | la nôtre | les nôtres | ours |
| le vôtre | la vôtre | les vôtres | yours |
| le leur | la leur | les leurs | theirs |

Possessive pronouns are used instead of a possessive adjective + noun. They agree in gender and in number with the noun they stand for, and not with the possessor (it is particularly important to remember this when translating 'his' and 'hers'):

> **j'aime bien ton appartement mais je préfère le mien**
> I quite like your flat, but I prefer mine

> **on prend quelle voiture? la mienne ou la tienne?**
> which car shall we take? mine or yours?

> **comment sont vos profs? les nôtres sont sympas**
> what are your teachers like? ours are nice

> **j'avais mon passeport mais Brigitte avait oublié le sien**
> I had my passport, but Brigitte had forgotten hers

> **j'ai gardé ma moto mais Paul a vendu la sienne**
> I've kept my motorbike but Paul has sold his

**à or de + possessive pronoun**

The prepositions **à** and **de** combine with the articles **le** and **les** in the usual way:

| à + le mien | → | au mien |
|-------------|---|---------|
| à + les miens | → | aux miens |
| à + les miennes | → | aux miennes |
| de + le mien | → | du mien |
| de + les miens | → | des miens |
| de + les miennes | → | des miennes |

**demande à tes parents, j'ai déjà parlé aux miens**
ask your parents, I've already spoken to mine

**leur appartement ressemble beaucoup au nôtre**
their flat is very similar to ours

**j'aime bien les chiens mais j'ai peur du tien**
I like dogs, but I'm afraid of yours

Note that after the verb **être**, the possessive pronoun is often replaced by **à** + emphatic pronoun (see p 88):

**à qui est cette écharpe? – elle est à moi**
whose scarf is this? – it's mine

**ce livre est à toi? – non, il est à elle**
is this book yours? – no, it's hers

**c'est à qui? à vous ou à lui?**
whose is this? yours or his?

# F. Relative Pronouns

## 1. Definition

Relative pronouns are words which introduce a relative clause. In the sentence:

> I bought the book which you recommended

'which' is the relative pronoun, 'which you recommended' is the relative clause and 'the book' is the antecedent (ie the noun to which the relative pronoun refers).

## 2. Forms

Relative pronouns are:

| | | | |
|---|---|---|---|
| qui | who/which | lequel | which |
| que | who(m)/which | dont | of which/whose |
| quoi | what | ce qui | what |
| où | where | ce que | what |

qui, que, quoi, lequel, ce qui and ce que can also be used as interrogative pronouns (see pp 73-6) and must not be confused with them.

## 3. Use

a) *QUI*

qui is used as the subject of a relative clause. It means:

i) 'who', 'that' (referring to people):

> **est-ce que tu connais le monsieur qui habite ici?**
> do you know the man who lives here?

> **ce n'est pas lui qui a menti**
> he's not the one who lied

ii) 'which', 'that' (referring to things):

> **tu as pris le journal qui était sur la télé?**
> did you take the paper which/that was on the TV?

93

### b) *QUE*

**que** (which contracts to **qu'** before a vowel or a silent **h**) is used as the object of a relative clause; it is often not translated. It means:

i) 'who(m)', 'that' (referring to people):

**la fille que j'aime ne m'aime pas**
the girl (that) I love doesn't love me

ii) 'which', 'that' (referring to things):

**j'ai perdu le briquet qu'il m'a offert**
I've lost the lighter (which/that) he gave me

### c) *qui* or *que*?

**qui** (subject) and **que** (object) are translated by the same words in English (who, which, that). To use the correct pronoun in French, it is essential to know whether a relative pronoun is the object or the subject of the relative clause:

i) when the verb of the relative clause has its own subject, the object pronoun **que** must be used:

**c'est un passe-temps que j'adore**
it's a pastime (that) I love *(the subject of 'adore' is 'je')*

ii) otherwise the relative pronoun is the subject of the verb in the relative clause and the subject pronoun **qui** must be used:

**j'ai trouvé un manteau qui me plaît**
I've found a coat that I like *(the subject of 'plaît' is 'qui')*

### d) *LEQUEL*

i) forms

**lequel** (which) has four different forms, as it must agree with the noun to which it refers:

|  | SINGULAR | PLURAL |  |
|---|---|---|---|
| MASCULINE | lequel | lesquels | } which |
| FEMININE | laquelle | lesquelles | |

**lequel** etc combines with the prepositions **à** and **de** as follows:

| | | |
|---|---|---|
| à + lequel | → | auquel |
| à + lesquels | → | auxquels |
| à + lesquelles | → | auxquelles |
| de + lequel | → | duquel |
| de + lesquels | → | desquels |
| de + lesquelles | → | desquelles |

**à + laquelle** and **de + laquelle** do not change.

**quels sont les sports auxquels tu t'intéresses?**
what sports are you interested *in*?

**voilà le village près duquel on campait**
here's the village which we camped near

ii) **qui** or **lequel** with a preposition?

When a relative pronoun follows a preposition, the pronoun used is either **qui** or **lequel**. In English, the relative pronoun is seldom used and the preposition is frequently placed after the verb or at the end of the sentence.

**qui** is generally used after a preposition when referring to people:

**où est la fille *avec* qui je dansais?**
where's the girl I was dancing *with*?

**montre-moi la personnne *à* qui tu as vendu ton vélo**
show me the person you sold your bike *to*

**lequel** is often used after a preposition when referring to things:

**l'immeuble *dans* lequel j'habite est très moderne**
the building (which) I live *in* is very modern

**je ne reconnais pas la voiture *avec* laquelle il est venu**
I don't recognize the car (which) he came *in*

**lequel** is also used when referring to persons after the prepositions **entre** (between) and **parmi** (among):

**elle observait les invités parmi lesquels elle ne reconnaissait personne**
she was watching the guests, none of whom she recognized

il y avait deux candidats, entre lesquels nous avons dû choisir
there were two candidates, between whom we had to choose

## e) DONT

**dont** is frequently used instead of **de qui, duquel** etc. It means:

### i) of which/of whom:

un métier dont il est fier
a job (which) he is proud of

Care must be taken with verbs that are normally followed by **de** + object: **de** is not always translated by 'of' in English, and is sometimes not translated at all (see section on verbal constructions pp 204-5):

voilà les choses *dont* j'ai besoin
here are the things (*which*) I need

les gens *dont* tu parles ne m'intéressent pas
I'm not interested in the people you're talking about

l'enfant *dont* elle s'occupe n'est pas le sien
the child she is looking *after* is not hers

### ii) whose

**dont** is also used to translate the English pronoun 'whose'. In French, the construction of the clause that follows **dont** differs from English in two ways:

▫ the noun which follows **dont** is used with the definite article (**le, la, les, l'**):

mon copain, dont *le* père a eu un accident
my friend, whose father had an accident

▫ the word order in French is **dont** + subject + verb + object:

je te présente Hélène, dont tu connais déjà le frère
this is Hélène, whose brother you already know

c'était dans une petite rue dont j'ai oublié le nom
it was in a small street the name of which I've forgotten

Note that **dont** cannot be used after a preposition:

une jolie maison, *près* de laquelle il y a un petit lac
a pretty house, *next* to which there is a small lake

## f) OÙ

i) **où** generally means 'where':

> **l'hôtel où on a logé était très confortable**
> the hotel where we stayed was very comfortable

ii) **où** often replaces a preposition + **lequel**, and means 'in/to/on/at which' etc:

> **c'est la maison où je suis né**
> that's the house in which/where I was born

> **une soirée où il a invité tous ses amis**
> a party to which he invited all his friends

iii) **où** is also used to translate 'when' after a noun referring to time:

> **le jour où**          **la fois où**          **le moment où**
> the day when          the time when          the moment when

> **tu te rappelles le soir où on a raté le dernier métro?**
> do you remember the evening when we missed the last train?

> **le jour où j'ai eu mon permis de conduire**
> the day when I got my driving licence

## g) CE QUI, CE QUE

**ce** is used before **qui** and **que** when the relative pronoun does not refer to a specific noun. Both **ce qui** and **ce que** mean 'that which', 'the thing which', and are usually translated by 'what':

i) **ce qui**

**ce qui** is followed by a verb without a subject (**qui** is the subject):

> **ce qui s'est passé ne vous regarde pas**
> what happened is none of your business

> **ce qui m'étonne, c'est sa patience**
> what surprises me is his patience

Note that in French, this structure requires a comma between the two clauses, and the second clause must be introduced by **c'est**/**c'était**/**ce sera** depending on the tense being used.

### ii) ce que

**ce que** (**ce qu'** before a vowel or a silent **h**) is followed by a verb with its own subject (**que** is the object):

**fais ce que tu veux**  
do what you want

**c'est ce qu'il a dit?**  
is that what he said?

**ce que vous me demandez est impossible**  
what you're asking me is impossible

### iii) tout ce qui/que

**tout** is used in front of **ce qui/que** in the sense of 'all that', 'everything that':

**c'est tout ce que je veux**  
that's all I want

**tout ce que tu as fait**  
everything you did

**tu n'as pas eu de mal; c'est tout ce qui compte**  
you weren't hurt; that's all that matters

### iv) ce qui/que are often used in indirect questions (see p 76):

**je ne sais pas ce qu'ils vont dire**  
I don't know what they'll say

v) when referring to a previous clause, **ce qui** and **ce que** are translated by 'which':

**elle est en retard, ce qui arrive souvent**  
she's late, which happens often

vi) **ce qui/que** are used with a preposition; **ce qui** is used as the subject of the verb in the relative clause and **ce que** is used as the object of the verb in the relative clause:

**ce n'est pas étonnant, après ce qui nous est arrivé**  
it's not surprising, after what happened to us

**il y a du vrai dans ce que vous dites**  
there is some truth in what you say

When a preposition is required by the verb in the relative clause, eg **penser à, s'expliquer sur, quoi** is used instead of **ce que** and comes after the preposition:

**c'est ce à quoi je pensais**  
that's what I was thinking about

**voici ce sur quoi il devra s'expliquer**
this is what he'll have to explain

**ce dont** is used instead of **de + ce que** when **de** is the preposition required by the verb in the relative clause, eg **avoir peur de, avoir besoin de**:

**c'est ce dont j'avais peur**
that's what I was afraid of

**tu as trouvé ce dont tu avais besoin?**
did you find what you needed?

# 7. VERBS

## A. Regular Conjugations

### 1. Conjugations

There are three main conjugations in French, which are determined by the infinitive endings. The first conjugation verbs, by far the largest category, end in **-er**, eg aim**er** and will be referred to as **-er** verbs; the second conjugation verbs end in **-ir**, eg fin**ir** and will be referred to as **-ir** verbs; the third conjugation verbs, the smallest category, end in **-re**, eg vend**re** and will be referred to as **-re** verbs.

### 2. Simple tenses

The simple tenses in French are:

- present
- imperfect
- future
- conditional
- past historic
- present subjunctive
- imperfect subjunctive

For the use of the different tenses, see pp 126-33.

### 3. Formation of tenses

The tenses are formed by adding the following endings to the stem of the verb (usually the stem of the infinitive) as set out in the following section:

a)   *PRESENT*: stem of the infinitive + the following endings:

| -er verbs | -ir verbs | -re verbs |
|---|---|---|
| -e, -es, -e, | -is, -is, -it, | -s, -s, ø, |
| -ons, -ez, -ent | -issons, -issez, | -ons, -ez, -ent |
|  | -issent |  |

| AIMER | FINIR | VENDRE |
|---|---|---|
| j'aime | je finis | je vends |
| tu aimes | tu finis | tu vends |
| il aime | il finit | il vend |
| elle aime | elle finit | elle vend |
| nous aimons | nous finissons | nous vendons |
| vous aimez | vous finissez | vous vendez |
| ils aiment | ils finissent | ils vendent |
| elles aiment | elles finissent | elles vendent |

b) *IMPERFECT*: stem of the first person plural of the present indicative (ie the 'nous' form minus -ons) + the following endings:

**-ais, -ais, -ait, -ions, -iez, -aient**

| j'aimais | je finissais | je vendais |
|---|---|---|
| tu aimais | tu finissais | tu vendais |
| il aimait | il finissait | il vendait |
| elle aimait | elle finissait | elle vendait |
| nous aimions | nous finissions | nous vendions |
| vous aimiez | vous finissiez | vous vendiez |
| ils aimaient | ils finissaient | ils vendaient |
| elles aimaient | elles finissaient | elles vendaient |

Note that the only irregular imperfect is **être**: **j'étais** etc.

c) *FUTURE*: infinitive + the following endings:

**-ai, -as, -a, -ons, -ez, -ont**

Note that verbs ending in **-re** drop the final **e** of the infinitive.

| j'aimerai | je finirai | je vendrai |
|---|---|---|
| tu aimeras | tu finiras | tu vendras |
| il aimera | il finira | il vendra |
| elle aimera | elle finira | elle vendra |
| nous aimerons | nous finirons | nous vendrons |
| vous aimerez | vous finirez | vous vendrez |
| ils aimeront | ils finiront | ils vendront |
| elles aimeront | elles finiront | elles vendront |

**d)** *CONDITIONAL* : infinitive + the following endings:

-ais, -ais, -ait, -ions, -iez, -aient

Note that verbs ending in **-re** drop the final **e** of the infinitive.

| | | |
|---|---|---|
| j'aimer**ais** | je finir**ais** | je vendr**ais** |
| tu aimer**ais** | tu finir**ais** | tu vendr**ais** |
| il aimer**ait** | il finir**ait** | il vendr**ait** |
| elle aimer**ait** | elle finir**ait** | elle vendr**ait** |
| nous aimer**ions** | nous finir**ions** | nous vendr**ions** |
| vous aimer**iez** | vous finir**iez** | vous vendr**iez** |
| ils aimer**aient** | ils finir**aient** | ils vendr**aient** |
| elles aimer**aient** | elles finir**aient** | elles vendr**aient** |

**e)** *PAST HISTORIC* : stem of the infinitive + the following endings:

| **-er** verbs | **-ir** verbs | **-re** verbs |
|---|---|---|
| -ai, -as, -a, | -is, -is, -it, | -is, -is, -it, |
| -âmes, -âtes, | -îmes, -îtes, | -îmes, -îtes, |
| -èrent | -irent | -irent |

| | | |
|---|---|---|
| j'aim**ai** | je fin**is** | je vend**is** |
| tu aim**as** | tu fin**is** | tu vend**is** |
| il aim**a** | il fin**it** | il vend**it** |
| elle aim**a** | elle fin**it** | elle vend**it** |
| nous aim**âmes** | nous fin**îmes** | nous vend**îmes** |
| vous aim**âtes** | vous fin**îtes** | vous vend**îtes** |
| ils aim**èrent** | ils fin**irent** | ils vend**irent** |
| elles aim**èrent** | elles fin**irent** | elles vend**irent** |

**f)** *PRESENT SUBJUNCTIVE* : stem of the first person plural of the present indicative (ie the '**nous**' form minus **-ons**) + the following endings:

-e, -es, -e, -ions, -iez, -ent

| | | |
|---|---|---|
| j'aim**e** | je finiss**e** | je vend**e** |
| tu aim**es** | tu finiss**es** | tu vend**es** |
| il aim**e** | il finiss**e** | il vend**e** |
| elle aim**e** | elle finiss**e** | elle vend**e** |
| nous aim**ions** | nous finiss**ions** | nous vend**ions** |
| vous aim**iez** | vous finiss**iez** | vous vend**iez** |
| ils aim**ent** | ils finiss**ent** | ils vend**ent** |
| elles aim**ent** | elles finiss**ent** | elles vend**ent** |

**g)** *IMPERFECT SUBJUNCTIVE*: stem of the first person singular of the past historic + the following endings:

| **-er** verbs | **-ir** verbs | **-re** verbs |
|---|---|---|
| -asse, -asses, -ât, | -isse, -isses, -ît, | -isse, -isses, -ît, |
| -assions, -assiez, | -issions, -issiez, | -issions, -issiez, |
| -assent | -issent | -issent |

| | | |
|---|---|---|
| j'aim**asse** | je fin**isse** | je vend**isse** |
| tu aim**asses** | tu fin**isses** | tu vend**isses** |
| il aim**ât** | il fin**ît** | il vend**ît** |
| elle aim**ât** | elle fin**ît** | elle vend**ît** |
| nous aim**assions** | nous fin**issions** | nous vend**issions** |
| vous aim**assiez** | vous fin**issiez** | vous vend**issiez** |
| ils aim**assent** | ils fin**issent** | ils vend**issent** |
| elles aim**assent** | elles fin**issent** | elles vend**issent** |

# B. Standard Spelling Irregularities

Spelling irregularities only affect **-er** verbs.

## 1. Verbs ending in -cer and -ger

a) Verbs ending in **-cer** require a cedilla under the **c** (**ç**) before an **a** or an **o** to preserve the soft sound of the **c**: eg **commencer** (to begin); **il commença** (he began).

b) Verbs ending in **-ger** require an **-e** after the **g** before an **a** or an **o** to preserve the soft sound of the **g**: eg **manger** (to eat); **je mangeais** (I was eating).

Changes to **-cer** and **-ger** verbs occur in the following tenses: present, imperfect, past historic, imperfect subjunctive and present participle.

| COMMENCER | MANGER |
|---|---|
| *PRESENT* | |
| je commence | je mange |
| tu commences | tu manges |
| il commence | il mange |
| elle commence | elle mange |
| nous **commençons** | nous **mangeons** |
| vous commencez | vous mangez |
| ils commencent | ils mangent |
| elles commencent | elles mangent |
| *IMPERFECT* | |
| je **commençais** | je **mangeais** |
| tu **commençais** | tu **mangeais** |
| il **commençait** | il **mangeait** |
| elle **commençait** | elle **mangeait** |
| nous commencions | nous mangions |
| vous commenciez | vous mangiez |
| ils **commençaient** | ils **mangeaient** |
| elles **commençaient** | elles **mangeaient** |

## PAST HISTORIC

| | |
|---|---|
| je commençai | je mangeai |
| tu commenças | tu mangeas |
| il commença | il mangea |
| elle commença | elle mangea |
| nous commençâmes | nous mangeâmes |
| vous commençâtes | vous mangeâtes |
| ils commencèrent | ils mangèrent |
| elles commencèrent | elles mangèrent |

## IMPERFECT SUBJUNCTIVE

| | |
|---|---|
| je commençasse | je mangeasse |
| tu commençasses | tu mangeasses |
| il commençât | il mangeât |
| elle commençât | elle mangeât |
| nous commençassions | nous mangeassions |
| vous commençassiez | vous mangeassiez |
| ils commençassent | ils mangeassent |
| elles commençassent | elles mangeassent |

## PRESENT PARTICIPLE

| | |
|---|---|
| commençant | mangeant |

## 2. Verbs with other -er endings

a) Verbs ending in **-eler**

Verbs ending in **-eler** double the **l** before a silent **e** (ie before **-e, -es, -ent** of the present indicative and subjunctive, and throughout the future and present conditional): eg **appeler** (to call).

| *PRESENT INDICATIVE* | *PRESENT SUBJUNCTIVE* |
|---|---|
| j'**appelle** | j'**appelle** |
| tu **appelles** | tu **appelles** |
| il **appelle** | il **appelle** |
| elle **appelle** | elle **appelle** |
| nous appelons | nous appelions |
| vous appelez | vous appeliez |
| ils **appellent** | ils **appellent** |
| elles **appellent** | elles **appellent** |

| *FUTURE* | *CONDITIONAL* |
|---|---|
| j'**appellerai** | j'**appellerais** |
| tu **appelleras** | tu **appellerais** |
| il **appellera** | il **appellerait** |
| elle **appellera** | elle **appellerait** |
| nous **appellerons** | nous **appellerions** |
| vous **appellerez** | vous **appelleriez** |
| ils **appelleront** | ils **appelleraient** |
| elles **appelleront** | elles **appelleraient** |

Note, however, that some verbs in **-eler**, including the following, are conjugated like **acheter** (see p 109):

| | |
|---|---|
| celer | to conceal |
| congeler | to (deep-)freeze |
| déceler | to detect, to reveal |
| dégeler | to defrost |
| geler | to freeze |
| harceler | to harass |
| marteler | to hammer |
| modeler | to model |
| peler | to peel |

**b)** Verbs ending in **-eter**

Verbs ending in **-eter** double the **t** before a silent **e** (ie before **-e, -es, -ent** of the present indicative and subjunctive, and throughout the future and conditional): eg **jeter** (to throw).

| PRESENT INDICATIVE | PRESENT SUBJUNCTIVE |
|---|---|
| je **jette** | je **jette** |
| tu **jettes** | tu **jettes** |
| il **jette** | il **jette** |
| elle **jette** | elle **jette** |
| nous jetons | nous jetions |
| vous jetez | vous jetiez |
| ils **jettent** | ils **jettent** |
| elles **jettent** | elles **jettent** |

| FUTURE | CONDITIONAL |
|---|---|
| je **jetterai** | je **jetterais** |
| tu **jetteras** | tu **jetterais** |
| il **jettera** | il **jetterait** |
| elle **jettera** | elle **jetterait** |
| nous **jetterons** | nous **jetterions** |
| vous **jetterez** | vous **jetteriez** |
| ils **jetteront** | ils **jetteraient** |
| elles **jetteront** | elles **jetteraient** |

Note, however, that some verbs in **-eter**, including the following, are conjugated like **acheter** (see p 109):

| crocheter | to pick *(a lock)* |
| fureter | to ferret about |
| haleter | to pant |
| racheter | to buy back |

c) Verbs ending in **-oyer** and **-uyer**

In verbs ending in **-oyer** and **-uyer** the **y** changes to **i** before a silent **e** (ie before **-e, -es, -ent** of the present indicative and subjunctive, and throughout the future and conditional): eg **employer** (to use) and **ennuyer** (to bore).

|  |  |
|---|---|
| *PRESENT INDICATIVE* | *PRESENT SUBJUNCTIVE* |
| j'emploie | j'emploie |
| tu emploies | tu emploies |
| il emploie | il emploie |
| elle emploie | elle emploie |
| nous employons | nous employions |
| vous employez | vous employiez |
| ils emploient | ils emploient |
| elles emploient | elles emploient |
| *FUTURE* | *CONDITIONAL* |
| j'emploierai | j'emploierais |
| tu emploieras | tu emploierais |
| il emploiera | il emploierait |
| elle emploiera | elle emploierait |
| nous emploierons | nous emploierions |
| vous emploierez | vous emploieriez |
| ils emploieront | ils emploieraient |
| elles emploieront | elles emploieraient |

Note that **envoyer** (to send) and **renvoyer** (to dismiss) have an irregular future and conditional: j'enverrai, j'enverrais; je renverrai, je renverrais.

d) Verbs ending in **-ayer**

In verbs ending in **-ayer**, eg **balayer** (to sweep), **payer** (to pay), **essayer** (to try), the change from **y** to **i** is optional:

| eg | je **balaie** | *or* | je **balaye** |
|---|---|---|---|
|  | je **paie** | *or* | je **paye** |
|  | j'**essaie** | *or* | j'**essaye** |

### e) Verbs in **e-** + consonant + **-er**

Verbs like **acheter, enlever, mener, peser** change the (last) **e** of the stem to **è** before a silent **e** (ie before **-e, -es, -ent** of the present indicative and subjunctive and throughout the future and conditional):

| *PRESENT INDICATIVE* | *PRESENT SUBJUNCTIVE* |
|---|---|
| j'**achète** | j'**achète** |
| tu **achètes** | tu **achètes** |
| il **achète** | il **achète** |
| elle **achète** | elle **achète** |
| nous achetons | nous achetions |
| vous achetez | vous achetiez |
| ils **achètent** | ils **achètent** |
| elles **achètent** | elles **achètent** |

| *FUTURE* | *CONDITIONAL* |
|---|---|
| j'**achèterai** | j'**achèterais** |
| tu **achèteras** | tu **achèterais** |
| il **achètera** | il **achèterait** |
| elle **achètera** | elle **achèterait** |
| nous **achèterons** | nous **achèterions** |
| vous **achèterez** | vous **achèteriez** |
| ils **achèteront** | ils **achèteraient** |
| elles **achèteront** | elles **achèteraient** |

Verbs conjugated like **acheter** include:

| | |
|---|---|
| **achever** to complete | **haleter** to pant |
| **amener** to bring | **harceler** to harass |
| **celer** to conceal | **lever** to lift |
| **crever** to burst | **marteler** to hammer |
| **crocheter** to pick *(lock)* | **mener** to lead |
| **élever** to raise | **modeler** to model |
| **emmener** to take away | **peler** to peel |
| **enlever** to remove | **peser** to weigh |
| **étiqueter** to label | **se promener** to go for a walk |
| **fureter** to ferret about | **semer** to sow |
| **geler** to freeze | **soulever** to lift |

# VERBS

## f) Verbs in **é-** + consonant + **-er**

Verbs like **espérer** (to hope) change **é** to **è** before a silent **e** in the present indicative and subjunctive. Note, however, that in the future and conditional **é** is retained.

| PRESENT INDICATIVE | PRESENT SUBJUNCTIVE |
|---|---|
| j'espère | j'espère |
| tu espères | tu espères |
| il espère | il espère |
| elle espère | elle espère |
| nous espérons | nous espérions |
| vous espérez | vous espériez |
| ils espèrent | ils espèrent |
| elles espèrent | elles espèrent |

| FUTURE | CONDITIONAL |
|---|---|
| j'espérerai | j'espérerais |
| tu espéreras | tu espérerais |
| il espérera | il espérerait |
| elle espérera | elle espérerait |
| nous espérerons | nous espérerions |
| vous espérerez | vous espéreriez |
| ils espéreront | ils espéreraient |
| elles espéreront | elles espéreraient |

Verbs conjugated like **espérer** include verbs in **-éder, -érer, -éter** etc:

| | |
|---|---|
| accéder | to accede to |
| céder | to yield |
| célébrer | to celebrate |
| compléter | to complete |
| considérer | to consider |
| décéder | to die |
| digérer | to digest |
| gérer | to manage |
| inquiéter | to worry |
| libérer | to free |
| opérer | to operate |
| pénétrer | to penetrate |

| | |
|---|---|
| persévérer | to persevere |
| posséder | to possess |
| précéder | to precede |
| préférer | to prefer |
| protéger | to protect |
| récupérer | to recover |
| refréner | to curb |
| régler | to rule |
| régner | to reign |
| répéter | to repeat, to rehearse |
| révéler | to reveal |
| sécher | to dry |
| succéder | to succeed |
| suggérer | to suggest |
| tolérer | to tolerate |

## C. Auxiliaries And The Formation Of Compound Tenses

### 1. Formation

a) The two auxiliary verbs **avoir** and **être** are used with the past participle of a verb to form compound tenses.

b) *The past participle*

The regular past participle is formed by taking the stem of the infinitive and adding the following endings:

| -er | -ir | -re |
|---|---|---|
| aim**(er)** + **é** | fin**(ir)** + **i** | vend**(re)** + **u** |
| aim**é** | fini | vend**u** |

For the agreement of past participles see pp 158-60.

c) *Compound tenses*

In French there are seven compound tenses: perfect, pluperfect, future perfect, past conditional (conditional perfect), past anterior, perfect subjunctive, pluperfect subjunctive.

### 2. Verbs conjugated with AVOIR

| *PERFECT* | *PLUPERFECT* |
|---|---|
| present of **avoir** + past participle | imperfect of **avoir** + past participle |
| j'ai aimé | j'avais aimé |
| tu as aimé | tu avais aimé |
| il a aimé | il avait aimé |
| elle a aimé | elle avait aimé |
| nous avons aimé | nous avions aimé |
| vous avez aimé | vous aviez aimé |
| ils ont aimé | ils avaient aimé |
| elles ont aimé | elles avaient aimé |

## FUTURE PERFECT

future of **avoir** +
past participle

j'aurai aimé
tu auras aimé
il aura aimé
elle aura aimé
nous aurons aimé
vous aurez aimé
ils auront aimé
elles auront aimé

## PAST ANTERIOR

past historic of **avoir** +
past participle

j'eus aimé
tu eus aimé
il eut aimé
elle eut aimé
nous eûmes aimé
vous eûtes aimé
ils eurent aimé
elles eurent aimé

## PERFECT SUBJUNCTIVE

present subjunctive of
**avoir** + past participle

j'aie aimé
tu aies aimé
il ait aimé
elle ait aimé
nous ayons aimé
vous ayez aimé
ils aient aimé
elles aient aimé

## PAST CONDITIONAL

conditional of **avoir** +
past participle

j'aurais aimé
tu aurais aimé
il aurait aimé
elle aurait aimé
nous aurions aimé
vous auriez aimé
ils auraient aimé
elles auraient aimé

## PLUPERFECT
## SUBJUNCTIVE

imperfect subjunctive of
**avoir** + past participle

j'eusse aimé
tu eusses aimé
il eût aimé
elle eût aimé
nous eussions aimé
vous eussiez aimé
ils eussent aimé
elles eussent aimé

### 3. Verbs conjugated with ÊTRE

*PERFECT*

present of **être** +
past participle

je suis arrivé(e)
tu es arrivé(e)
il est arrivé
elle est arrivée
nous sommes arrivé(e)s
vous êtes arrivé(e)(s)
ils sont arrivés
elles sont arrivées

*FUTURE PERFECT*

future of **être** +
past participle

je serai arrivé(e)
tu seras arrivé(e)
il sera arrivé
elle sera arrivée
nous serons arrivé(e)s
vous serez arrivé(e)(s)
ils seront arrivés
elles seront arrivées

*PAST ANTERIOR*

past historic of **être** +
past participle

je fus arrivé(e)
tu fus arrivé(e)
il fut arrivé
elle fut arrivée
nous fûmes arrivé(e)s
vous fûtes arrivé(e)(s)
ils furent arrivés
elles furent arrivées

*PLUPERFECT*

imperfect of **être** +
past participle

j'étais arrivé(e)
tu étais arrivé(e)
il était arrivé
elle était arrivée
nous étions arrivé(e)s
vous étiez arrivé(e)(s)
ils étaient arrivés
elles étaient arrivées

*PAST CONDITIONAL*

conditional of **être** +
past participle

je serais arrivé(e)
tu serais arrivé(e)
il serait arrivé
elle serait arrivée
nous serions arrivé(e)s
vous seriez arrivé(e)(s)
ils seraient arrivés
elles seraient arrivées

| *PERFECT SUBJUNCTIVE* | *PLUPERFECT SUBJUNCTIVE* |
|---|---|
| present subjunctive of **être** + past participle | imperfect subjunctive of **être** + past participle |
| je sois arrivé(e) | je fusse arrivé(e) |
| tu sois arrivé(e) | tu fusses arrivé(e) |
| il soit arrivé | il fût arrivé |
| elle soit arrivée | elle fût arrivée |
| nous soyons arrivé(e)s | nous fussions arrivé(e)s |
| vous soyez arrivé(e)(s) | vous fussiez arrivé(e)(s) |
| ils soient arrivés | ils fussent arrivés |
| elles soient arrivées | elles fussent arrivées |

## 4. AVOIR or ÊTRE?

**a)** *Verbs conjugated with* **avoir**

The compound tenses of most verbs are formed with **avoir**:

| | |
|---|---|
| j'ai marqué un but | elle a dansé toute la nuit |
| I scored a goal | she danced all night |

**b)** *Verbs conjugated with* **être**

i) all reflexive verbs (see p 119):

**je me suis baigné**
I had a bath

ii) the following verbs (mainly of motion):

| | |
|---|---|
| aller | to go |
| arriver | to arrive |
| descendre | to go/come down |
| entrer | to go/come in |
| monter | to go/come up |
| mourir | to die |
| naître | to be born |
| partir | to leave |
| passer | to go through, to drop in |
| rester | to remain |

| retourner | to return |
| sortir | to go/come out |
| tomber | to fall |
| venir | to come |

and most of their compounds:

| revenir | to come back |
| devenir | to become |
| parvenir | to reach, to manage to |
| rentrer | to return home |
| remonter | to go up again |
| redescendre | to go down again |

Note, however, that **prévenir** (to warn) and **subvenir** (to provide for) are conjugated with **avoir**:

**je t'avais prévenu!**
I did warn you!

**elle avait subvenu à toutes les dépenses**
she met all the expenses

Note too that **passer** can also be conjugated with **avoir**:

**il a passé par Paris**
he went via Paris

Some of the verbs listed above can take a direct object. In such cases they are conjugated with **avoir** and will have a different meaning:

| descendre | to take/bring down, to go down *(the stairs, a slope)* |
| monter | to take/bring up, to go up *(the stairs, a slope)* |
| rentrer | to take/bring/put in |
| retourner | to turn over |
| sortir | to take/bring out |

**les élèves sont sortis à midi**
the pupils came out at midday

**les élèves ont sorti leurs livres**
the pupils took out their books

**elle n'est pas encore descendue**
she hasn't come down yet

**elle a descendu un vieux tableau du grenier**
she brought an old painting down from the loft

**elle a descendu l'escalier**
she came down the stairs

**les prisonniers sont montés sur le toit**
the prisoners climbed on to the roof

**le garçon a monté les bouteilles de vin de la cave**
the waiter brought the bottles of wine up from the cellar

**nous sommes rentrés tard**
we got home late

**j'ai rentré la voiture dans le garage**
I put the car in the garage

**je serais retourné à Paris**
I would have returned to Paris

**le jardinier a retourné le sol**
the gardener turned over the soil

**ils sont sortis de la piscine**
they got out of the swimming pool

**il a sorti les mains de ses poches**
he took his hands out of his pockets

## D. Reflexive Verbs

### 1. Definition

Reflexive verbs are so called because they 'reflect' the action back onto the subject. Reflexive verbs are always accompanied by a reflexive pronoun, eg in the following sentence:

I look at myself in the mirror

'myself' is the reflexive pronoun.

| | |
|---|---|
| **je lave la voiture**<br>I'm washing the car | **je _me_ lave**<br>I'm washing _myself_ |
| **j'ai couché le bébé**<br>I put the baby to bed | **je _me_ suis couché**<br>I went to bed (I put _myself_ to bed) |

### 2. Reflexive pronouns

They are:

| PERSON | SINGULAR | PLURAL |
|---|---|---|
| 1st | **me (m')**<br>myself | **nous**<br>ourselves |
| 2nd | **te (t')**<br>yourself | **vous**<br>yourself/selves |
| 3rd | **se (s')**<br>himself, herself, itself, oneself | **se (s')**<br>themselves |

_Note:_

a) **m'**, **t'** and **s'** are used instead of **me, te** and **se** in front of a vowel or a silent **h**:

**tu t'amuses? – non, je m'ennuie**
are you enjoying yourself? – no, I'm bored

**il s'habille dans la salle de bain**
he gets dressed in the bathroom

b) French reflexive pronouns are often not translated in English:

| **je me demande si …** | **ils se moquent de moi** |
|---|---|
| I wonder if … | they're making fun of me |

**c)** Plural reflexive pronouns can also be used to express reciprocal actions; in this case they are translated by 'each other' or 'one another':

| | |
|---|---|
| **nous nous détestons** | **ils ne se parlent pas** |
| we hate one another | they're not talking to each other |

**d)** **se** can mean 'ourselves' or 'each other' when it is used with the pronoun **on** meaning 'we' (see p 71):

| | |
|---|---|
| **on s'est perdu** | **on se connaît** |
| we got lost | we know each other |

## 3. Position of reflexive pronouns

Reflexive pronouns are placed immediately before the verb, except in positive commands, where they follow the verb and are linked to it by a hyphen:

| | |
|---|---|
| **tu te dépêches?** | **dépêchons-nous!** |
| will you hurry up? | let's hurry! |
| **ne t'inquiète pas** | **ne vous fiez pas à lui** |
| don't worry | don't trust him |

Note that reflexive pronouns change to emphatic (disjunctive) pronouns in positive commands:

| | |
|---|---|
| **elle doit se reposer** | **repose-toi** |
| she needs to rest | have a rest |

## 4. Conjugation of reflexive verbs

**a)** *Simple tenses*

These are conjugated in the same way as non-reflexive verbs, except that a reflexive pronoun is used.

**b)** *Compound tenses*

These are conjugated using the auxiliary **être** followed by the past participle of the verb.

A full conjugation table is given on p 187.

## 5. Agreement of the past participle

a) In most cases, the reflexive pronoun is a direct object and the past participle of the verb agrees in number and in gender with the reflexive pronoun:

**il s'est trompé**
he made a mistake

**elle s'est endormie**
she fell asleep

**ils se sont excusés**
they apologized

**elles se sont assises**
they sat down

b) When the reflexive pronoun is used as an indirect object, the past participle does not change:

**nous nous sommes écrit**
we wrote to each other

**elle se l'est acheté**
she bought it for herself

**elles se sont parlé**
they spoke to each other

**les années se sont succédé**
one year followed another

When the reflexive verb has a direct object, the reflexive pronoun is the indirect object of the reflexive verb and the past participle does not agree with it:

**Caroline s'est tordu la cheville**
Caroline sprained her ankle

**vous vous êtes lavé les mains, les filles?**
did you wash your hands, girls?

**elles se sont égratigné les genoux**
they scratched their knees

## 6. Common reflexive verbs

| | | |
|---|---|---|
| **s'en aller**<br>to go away | **s'éloigner (de)**<br>to move away<br>(from) | **se moquer de**<br>to laugh at |
| **s'amuser**<br>to have fun | **s'endormir**<br>to fall asleep | **s'occuper de**<br>to take care of |
| **s'appeler**<br>to be called | **s'ennuyer**<br>to be bored | **se passer**<br>to happen |

**s'approcher (de)**
to come near

**s'arrêter**
to stop

**s'asseoir**
to sit down

**s'attendre à**
to expect

**se baigner**
to have a bath

**se battre**
to fight

**se blesser**
to hurt oneself

**se coucher**
to go to bed

**se débarrasser de**
to get rid of

**se demander**
to wonder

**se dépêcher**
to hurry

**se déshabiller**
to undress

**se diriger vers**
to move towards

**s'étonner (de)**
to be surprised (at)

**s'excuser (de)**
to apologize (for)

**se fâcher**
to get angry/fall out

**s'écrier**
to cry out/exclaim

**s'habiller**
to get dressed

**se hâter**
to hurry

**s'inquiéter**
to worry

**s'installer**
to settle down

**se laver**
to wash

**se lever**
to get up

**se mêler de**
to meddle with

**se mettre à**
to start

**se mettre en route**
to set off

**se passer de**
to do without

**se promener**
to go for a walk

**se rappeler**
to remember

**se raser**
to shave

**se renseigner**
to make enquiries

**se ressembler**
to look alike

**se retourner**
to turn round

**se réveiller**
to wake up

**se sauver**
to run away

**se souvenir (de)**
to remember

**se taire**
to be/keep quiet

**se tromper**
to be mistaken

**se trouver**
to be (situated)

# E. Impersonal Verbs

## 1. Conjugation

Impersonal verbs are used only in the third person singular and in the infinitive. The subject is always the impersonal pronoun **il** (= it).

| | |
|---|---|
| **il neige**<br>it's snowing | **il y a du brouillard**<br>it's foggy |

## 2. List of impersonal verbs

a) *verbs describing the weather:*

i) **faire** + adjective:

| | |
|---|---|
| **il fait beau/chaud**<br>it's fine/warm | **il fait frais/froid**<br>it's cool/cold |
| **il fera beau demain**<br>the weather will be good tomorrow | **il va faire très froid**<br>it will be very cold |

ii) **faire** + noun:

| | |
|---|---|
| **il fait beau temps**<br>the weather is nice | **il fait mauvais temps**<br>the weather is bad |
| **il fait jour**<br>it's daylight | **il fait nuit**<br>it's dark |

iii) other impersonal verbs and verbs used impersonally to describe the weather:

| | | |
|---|---|---|
| il gèle | (geler) | it's freezing |
| il grêle | (grêler) | it's hailing |
| il neige | (neiger) | it's snowing |
| il pleut | (pleuvoir) | it's raining |
| il tonne | (tonner) | there's thunder |

Note that some of these verbs may be used personally:

| | |
|---|---|
| **je gèle** | I'm freezing |

iv) **il y a** + noun:

**il y a des nuages**       it's cloudy
**il y a du brouillard**    it's foggy
**il y a du verglas**       it's icy

**b)** *être*

i) **il est** + noun:

**il est cinq heures**       **il était une fois un géant**
it's five o'clock            once upon a time there was a
                             giant

ii) **il est** + adjective + **de** + infinitive:

**il est difficile de**      it's difficult to
**il est facile de**         it's easy to
**il est nécessaire de**     it's necessary to
**il est inutile de**        it's useless to
**il est possible de**       it's possible to

**il est difficile d'en parler**
it's difficult to talk about it

Note that the indirect object pronoun in French corresponds to the English 'for me', 'for him' etc:

**il m'est difficile d'en parler**
it's difficult for me to talk about it

iii) **il est** + adjective + **que**:

**il est douteux que**       it's doubtful that
**il est évident que**       it's clear that
**il est possible que**      it's possible that
**il est probable que**      it's probable that
**il est peu probable que**  it's unlikely that
**il est vrai que**          it's true that

Note that **que** may be followed by the indicative or the subjunctive (see p 126):

**il est probable qu'il ne viendra pas**
he probably won't come

il est peu probable qu'il vienne
it's unlikely that he'll come

**c)** *arriver, se passer (to happen)*

il est arrivé une chose curieuse
a strange thing happened

que se passe-t-il?
what's happening?

**d)** *exister (to exist), rester (to remain), manquer (to be missing)*

il existe trois exemplaires de ce livre
there are three copies of this book

il me restait un euro
I had one euro left

il me manque 4 euros
I am 4 euros short

**e)** *paraître, sembler (to seem)*

il paraîtrait/semblerait qu'il ait changé d'avis
it would appear that he has changed his mind

il paraît qu'il va se marier
it seems he's going to get married

il me semble que le professeur s'est trompé
it seems to me that the teacher has made a mistake

**f)** *other common impersonal verbs*

i) **s'agir** (to be a matter of) may be followed by a noun, a pronoun or an infinitive:

il s'agit de ton avenir
it's about your future

de quoi s'agit-il?
what's it about?

il s'agit de trouver le coupable
we must find the culprit

ii) **falloir** (to be necessary) may be followed by a noun, an infinitive or the subjunctive:

il faut deux heures pour aller à Paris
it takes two hours to get to Paris

il me faut plus de temps
I need more time

il faudra rentrer plus tôt ce soir
we'll have to come home earlier tonight

**il faut que tu parles à Papa**
you have to speak to Dad

iii) **suffire** (to be enough) may be followed by a noun, an infinitive or the subjunctive:

**il suffit de peu de chose pour être heureux**
it doesn't take much to be happy

**il suffit de passer le pont**
you only have to cross the bridge

**il suffira qu'ils te donnent le numéro de téléphone**
they will only have to give you the telephone number

iv) **valoir mieux** (to be better) may be followed by an infinitive or the subjunctive:

**il vaudrait mieux prendre le car**
it would be better to take the coach

**il vaut mieux que vous ne sortiez pas seule le soir**
you'd better not go out alone at night

## F. Tenses

For the formation of the different tenses, see pp 100-3 and 112-5.

Note that French has no continuous tenses (as in 'I am eating', 'I was going', 'I will be arriving'). The 'be' and '-ing' parts of English continuous tenses are not translated as separate words. Instead, the equivalent tense is used in French:

| | |
|---|---|
| **je mange**<br>I am eating | **je mangerai**<br>I will be eating |

### 1. PRESENT

The present is used to describe what someone does/something that happens regularly, or what someone is doing/something that is happening at the time of speaking.

a) *regular actions*

**il travaille dans un bureau**
he works in an office

**je lis rarement le journal**
I seldom read the paper

b) *continuous actions*

**ne le dérangez pas, il travaille**
don't disturb him, he's working

**je ne peux pas venir, je garde mon petit frère**
I can't come, I'm looking after my little brother

Note that the continuous nature of the action can also be expressed by using the phrase **être en train de** (to be in the process of) + infinitive:

**je suis en train de cuisiner**
I'm (busy) cooking

c) *immediate future*

**je pars demain**
I'm leaving tomorrow

However, the present cannot be used after **quand** and other conjunctions of time when the future is implied (see p 129):

> **je le ferai quand j'aurai le temps**
> I'll do it when I have the time

d) *general truths*

> **la vie est dure**
> life is hard

## 2. IMPERFECT

The imperfect is a past tense used to express what someone was doing or what someone used to do, or to describe something in the past. The imperfect refers particularly to something that *continued* over a period of time, as opposed to something that happened at a specific point in time.

a) *continuous actions*

the imperfect describes an action that was happening, often when something else took place:

> **il prenait un bain quand le téléphone a sonné**
> he was having a bath when the phone rang

> **excuse-moi, je pensais à autre chose**
> I'm sorry, I was thinking of something else

Note that the continuous nature of the action can be emphasized by using **être en train de** + infinitive:

> **j'étais en train de faire le ménage**
> I was (busy) doing the housework

b) *regular actions in the past*

> **je le voyais souvent quand il habitait dans le quartier**
> I used to see him often when he lived in this area

> **quand il était plus jeune il voyageait beaucoup**
> when he was younger he used to travel a lot

c) *description in the past*

> **il faisait beau ce jour-là**
> the weather was good that day

> **c'était formidable !**
> it was great!

> **elle portait une robe bleue**
> she wore a blue dress

> **elle donnait sur la rue**
> it looked onto the street

## 3. PERFECT

The perfect tense is a compound past tense, used to express *single* actions which have been completed. What someone did, has done or has been doing, or something that has happened or has been happening are all expressed using the perfect tense:

**je l'ai envoyé lundi**
I sent it on Monday

**on est sorti hier soir**
we went out last night

**tu t'es bien amusé?**
did you have a good time?

**je ne l'ai pas vu de toute la journée**
I haven't seen him all day

**j'ai lu toute la journée**
I've been reading all day

**tu as déjà mangé?**
have you eaten?

In English, the simple past ('did', 'went', 'prepared') is used to describe both single and repeated actions in the past. In French, the perfect only describes single actions in the past, while repeated actions are expressed by the imperfect (they are sometimes signposted by 'used to'). Thus 'I went' should be translated 'j'allais' or 'je suis allé' depending on the nature of the action:

**après dîner, je suis allé en ville**
after dinner I went into town

**l'an dernier, j'allais plus souvent au théâtre**
last year I went to the theatre more often

## 4. PAST HISTORIC

This tense is used in the same way as the perfect tense, to describe a single, completed action in the past (what someone did or something that happened). It is a literary tense, not common in everyday spoken French; it is found mainly as a narrative tense in written form:

**le piéton ne vit pas arriver la voiture**
the pedestrian didn't see the car coming

## 5. PLUPERFECT

This compound tense is used to express what someone had done/had been doing or something that had happened or had been happening:

**il n'avait pas voulu aller avec eux**
he hadn't wanted to go with them

**elle était essoufflée parce qu'elle avait couru**
she was out of breath because she'd been running

However, the pluperfect is not used as in English with **depuis** (for, since), or with **venir de** + infinitive (to have just done something). For details see pp 130-3:

**il neigeait depuis une semaine**
it had been snowing for a week

**les pompiers venaient d'arriver**
the firemen had just arrived

## 6. FUTURE

This tense is used to express what someone will do or will be doing or something that will happen or will be happening:

**je ferai la vaisselle demain**          **j'arriverai tard**
I'll do the dishes tomorrow                I'll be arriving late

Note that the future and not the present, as in English, is used in time clauses introduced by **quand** (when) or other conjunctions of time where the future is implied (see p 129):

**il viendra quand il le pourra**
he'll come when he can

French makes frequent use of **aller** + infinitive (to be about to do something) to express the immediate future:

**je vais vous expliquer ce qui s'est passé**
I'll explain (to you) what happened

**il va déménager la semaine prochaine**
he's moving house next week

## 7. FUTURE PERFECT

This compound tense is used to describe what someone will have done or will have been doing in the future or to describe something that will have happened in the future:

**j'aurai bientôt fini**
I will soon have finished

In particular, it is used instead of the English perfect in time clauses introduced by **quand** or other conjunctions of time where the future is implied (see p 129):

**appelle-moi quand tu auras fini**
call me when you've finished

**on rentrera dès qu'on aura fait les courses**
we'll come back as soon as we've done the shopping

## 8. PAST ANTERIOR

This tense is used instead of the pluperfect to express an action that preceded another action in the past (ie a past in the past). It is usually introduced by a conjunction of time (translated by 'when', 'as soon as', 'after' etc) and the main verb is in the past historic:

**il se coucha dès qu'ils furent partis**
he went to bed as soon as they'd left

**à peine eut-elle raccroché que le téléphone sonna**
she'd hardly hung up when the telephone rang

## 9. Use of tenses with 'depuis' (for, since)

a) The present must be used instead of the perfect to describe actions which started in the past and are still continuing:

**il habite ici depuis trois ans**
he's been living here for three years

**elle t'attend depuis ce matin**
she's been waiting for you since this morning

Note, however, that the perfect, not the present, is used when the clause is negative or when the action has been completed:

**il n'a pas pris de vacances depuis longtemps**
he hasn't taken any holidays for a long time

**j'ai fini depuis un bon moment**
I've been finished for quite a while

*Note:*

i) **il y a … que** or **voilà … que** are also used with the present tense to translate 'for':

it's been ringing for ten minutes
**ça sonne depuis dix minutes**
**il y a dix minutes que ça sonne**
**voilà dix minutes que ça sonne**

ii) **depuis que** is used when 'since' introduces a clause, ie when there is a verb following **depuis**:

**elle dort depuis que vous êtes partis**
she's been sleeping since you left

iii) Do not confuse **depuis** (for, since) and **pendant** (for, during): **depuis** refers to the starting point of an action which is still going on and **pendant** refers to the duration of an action which is over and is used with the perfect:

**il vit ici depuis deux mois**
he's been living here for two months

**il a vécu ici pendant deux mois**
he lived here for two months

b) The imperfect must be used instead of the pluperfect to describe an action which had started in the past and was still going on at a given time:

**elle le connaissait depuis son enfance**
she had known him since her childhood

**il attendait depuis trois heures quand on est arrivé**
he had been waiting for three hours when we arrived

Note, however, that if the sentence is negative or if the action has been completed, the pluperfect and not the imperfect is used:

**je n'étais pas allé au théâtre depuis des années**
I hadn't been to the theatre for years

**il était parti depuis peu**
he'd been gone for a short while

*Note:*

i) **il y avait … que** + imperfect is also used to translate 'for':

she'd been living alone for a long time
**elle habitait seule depuis longtemps**
**il y avait longtemps qu'elle habitait seule**

ii) **depuis que** is used when 'since' introduces a clause; if it describes an action which was still going on at the time, it can be followed by the imperfect, otherwise it is followed by the pluperfect:

**il pleuvait depuis que nous étions en vacances**
it had been raining since we had been on holiday

**il pleuvait depuis que nous étions arrivés**
it had been raining since we arrived

iii) Do not confuse **depuis** and **pendant**: **depuis** refers to the starting point of an action which is still going on and **pendant** refers to the duration of an action which is over; **pendant** is used with the pluperfect:

**j'y travaillais depuis un an**
I had been working there for a year

**j'y avais travaillé pendant un an**
I had worked there for a year

## 10. Use of tenses with 'venir de'

**venir de** + infinitive means 'to have just done'.

**a)** If it describes something that has just happened, it is used in the present instead of the perfect:

**l'avion vient d'arriver**          **je viens de te le dire!**
the plane has just arrived          I've just told you!

**b)** If it describes something that had just happened, it is used in the imperfect instead of the pluperfect:

132

le film venait de commencer | je venais de rentrer
the film had just started | I'd just got home

## 11. Use of tenses after conjunctions of time

| quand | when |
| tant que | as long as |
| dès/aussitôt que | as soon as |
| lorsque | when |
| pendant que | while |

Verbs which follow these conjunctions must be used in the following tenses:

**a)** *future instead of present:*

> je te téléphonerai quand je serai prêt
> I'll phone you when I'm ready

> elle ira le voir dès qu'elle le pourra
> she'll go to see him as soon as she can

**b)** *future perfect instead of perfect* when the future is implied:

> on rentrera dès qu'on aura fini les courses
> we'll come back as soon as we've done the shopping

> je t'appellerai dès qu'il sera arrivé
> I'll call you as soon as he's arrived

**c)** *conditional present/perfect instead of perfect/pluperfect* in indirect speech:

> il a dit qu'il sortirait quand il aurait fini
> he said that he would come out when he had finished

For the tenses of the subjunctive and conditional, see pp 134-8 and 141-2.

# G. Moods

## 1. THE SUBJUNCTIVE

In everyday spoken French, the only two subjunctive tenses that are used are the present and the perfect. The imperfect and the pluperfect subjunctive are found mainly in literature or in texts of a formal nature.

The subjunctive is always preceded by the conjunction **que** and is used in subordinate clauses when the subject of the subordinate clause is different from the subject of the main verb.

Some clauses introduced by **que** take the indicative. The subjunctive must be used after the following:

**a)** Verbs of emotion

| | |
|---|---|
| **être content que** | to be pleased that |
| **être désolé que** | to be sorry that |
| **être étonné que** | to be surprised that |
| **être heureux que** | to be happy that |
| **être surpris que** | to be surprised that |
| **être triste que** | to be sad that |
| **avoir peur que … ne** | to be afraid/to fear that |
| **craindre que … ne** | to be afraid/to fear that |
| **regretter que** | to be sorry that |

**ils étaient contents que j'aille les voir**
they were pleased (that) I went to visit them

**je serais très étonné qu'il mente**
I would be very surprised if he was lying

**je regrette que tu ne puisses pas y aller**
I'm sorry (that) you can't go

Note that **ne** is used after several verbs in the subjunctive mood but it does not have a negative meaning in itself and is not translated in English:

**je crains que l'avion *ne* soit en retard**
I'm afraid (that) the plane will be late

**j'ai bien peur qu'il *ne* soit déjà trop tard**
I'm very much afraid (that) it's already too late

**pour éviter que la situation *ne* s'aggrave**
to prevent the situation from getting any worse

**b)** Verbs of wishing and willing:

| | |
|---|---|
| **aimer que** | to like |
| **désirer que** | to wish (that) |
| **préférer que** | to prefer (that) |
| **souhaiter que** | to wish (that) |
| **vouloir que** | to want |

Note that in English, such verbs are often used in the following type of construction: verb of willing + object + infinitive (eg I'd like you to listen); this type of construction is impossible in French, where a subjunctive clause has to be used:

**je souhaite que tu réussisses**
I hope you will succeed

**il aimerait que je lui écrive plus souvent**
he'd like me to write to him more often

**voulez-vous que je vous y amène en voiture?**
would you like me to drive you there?

**préférez-vous que je rappelle demain?**
would you rather I called back tomorrow?

**c)** Impersonal constructions (expressing necessity, possibility, doubt, denial, preference):

| | |
|---|---|
| **il faut que** | it is necessary (that) *(must)* |
| **il est nécessaire que** | it is necessary that *(must)* |
| **il est important que** | it is important (that) |
| **il est possible que** | it is possible that *(may)* |
| **il se peut que** | it is possible that *(may)* |
| **il est impossible que** | it is impossible (that) *(can't)* |
| **il est douteux que** | it is doubtful whether |
| **il est peu probable que** | it is unlikely that |
| **il semble que** | it seems (that) |
| **il est préférable que** | it is preferable (that) |
| **il vaut mieux que** | it is better (that) *(had better)* |
| **c'est dommage que** | it is a pity (that) |

Note that these expressions may be used in any appropriate tense:

**il faut absolument que je le leur dise**
I simply must tell them

**il était important que tu le saches**
it was important that you should know

**il se pourrait qu'elle change d'avis**
she might change her mind

**il est peu probable qu'ils s'y intéressent**
they're unlikely to be interested in that

**il semble qu'elle ait raison**
she appears to be right

**il vaudrait mieux que tu ne promettes rien**
you'd better not promise anything

**c'est dommage que vous vous soyez manqués**
it's a pity you missed each other

**d)** Some verbs and impersonal constructions expressing doubt or uncertainty (mainly used negatively or interrogatively):

| | |
|---|---|
| **douter que** | to doubt (that) |
| **(ne pas) croire que** | (not) to believe (that) |
| **(ne pas) penser que** | (not) to think (that) |
| **(ne pas) être sûr que** | (not) to be sure that |
| **il n'est pas certain que** | it isn't certain that |
| **il n'est pas évident que** | it isn't obvious that |
| **il n'est pas sûr que** | it isn't certain that |
| **il n'est pas vrai que** | it isn't true that |

**je doute fort qu'il veuille t'aider**
I very much doubt whether he'll want to help you

**croyez-vous qu'il y ait des places libres?**
do you think there are any seats available?

**on n'était pas sûr que ce soit le bon endroit**
we weren't sure that it was the right place

**il n'était pas certain qu'elle puisse gagner**
it wasn't certain whether she could win

**e) attendre que** (to wait until someone does something or something happens, to wait for someone to do something or for something to happen):

> **attendons qu'il revienne**
> let's wait until he comes back

**f)** Some subordinating conjunctions:

| | |
|---|---|
| **bien que** | although |
| **quoique** | although |
| **sans que** | without |
| **pour que** | so that |
| **afin que** | so that |
| **à condition que** | provided that |
| **pourvu que** | provided that |
| **jusqu'à ce que** | until |
| **en attendant que** | until |
| **avant que … (ne)** | before |
| **à moins que … (ne)** | unless |
| **de peur que … ne** | for fear that |
| **de crainte que … ne** | for fear that |
| **de sorte que** | so that |
| **de façon que** | so that |
| **de manière que** | so that |

Note that when **ne** is shown in brackets, it may follow the conjunction, although it is seldom used in spoken French; it does not have a negative meaning, and is not translated in English.

> **il est allé travailler bien qu'il soit malade**
> he went to work although he was ill

> **elle est entrée sans que je la voie**
> she came in without me seeing her

> **voilà de l'argent pour que tu puisses aller au cinéma**
> here's some money so that you can go to the cinema

> **d'accord, pourvu que tu me promettes de ne pas le répéter**
> all right, as long as you promise not to tell anyone

> **tu l'as revu avant qu'il (ne) parte?**
> did you see him again before he left?

**je le ferai demain, à moins que ce (ne) soit urgent**
I'll do it tomorrow, unless it's urgent

**elle n'a pas fait de bruit de peur qu'il ne se réveille**
she didn't make any noise in case he woke

**parle moins fort de sorte qu'elle ne nous entende pas**
talk more quietly so that she doesn't hear us

Note that when **de façon/manière que** (so that) expresses a result, as opposed to a purpose, the indicative is used instead of the subjunctive:

**il a fait du bruit de sorte qu'elle l'a entendu**
he made some noise, and as a result she heard him

g) A superlative or adjectives like **premier** (first), **dernier** (last), **seul** (only) followed by **qui** or **que**:

**c'était le coureur le plus rapide que j'aie jamais vu**
he was the fastest runner I ever saw

Note, however, that the indicative is used with a statement of fact rather than the expression of an opinion:

**c'est lui qui me l'a dit**
it was he who told me

h) Negative and indefinite pronouns (eg **rien, personne, quelqu'un**) followed by **qui** or **que**:

**je ne connais personne qui fasse aussi bien les crêpes**
I don't know anyone who can make such good crêpes

**il n'y a aucune chance qu'il réussisse**
he hasn't got a chance of succeeding

**ils cherchent quelqu'un qui puisse garder le bébé**
they're looking for someone who can look after the baby

Note, however, that the subjunctive is not used if the verbs in both clauses have the same subject. The infinitive will be used in the subordinate clause instead, sometimes introduced by a preposition (**à** or **de**) (see pp 146-52).

**a) de** + infinitive replaces the subjunctive after:

i) verbs of emotion:

> **j'ai été étonné d'apprendre la nouvelle**
> I was surprised to hear the news

> **il regrette de ne pas être arrivé plus tôt**
> he's sorry he didn't arrive earlier

> **tu as peur de ne pas avoir assez d'argent?**
> are you worried you won't have enough money?

ii) **attendre** (to wait) and **douter** (to doubt):

> **j'attendrai d'avoir bu mon café**
> I'll wait until I've drunk my coffee

iii) most impersonal constructions:

> **il serait préférable de les en informer tout de suite**
> it would be better to let them know immediately

> **il est indispensable de parler une langue étrangère**
> it's essential to be able to speak a foreign language

iv) most conjunctions:

> **il est resté dans la voiture afin de ne pas se mouiller**
> he stayed in the car so as not to get wet

> **j'ai lu avant de m'endormir**
> I read before falling asleep

> **tu peux sortir à condition de rentrer avant minuit**
> you can go out, as long as you're back before midnight

**b) à** + infinitive replaces the subjunctive after:

i) **de façon/manière**

> **mets la liste sur la table de manière à ne pas l'oublier**
> put the list on the table so that you won't forget it

ii) **premier, seul, dernier**

> **il a été le seul à s'excuser**
> he was the only one who apologized

**c)** The infinitive without any linking preposition replaces the subjunctive after:

i) verbs of wishing and willing:

**je voudrais sortir avec toi**
I'd like to go out with you

ii) **il faut, il vaut mieux**:

**il vous faudra prendre des chèques de voyage**
you'll have to take some traveller's cheques

**il lui a fallu recommencer à zéro**
he had to start all over again

**il vaudrait mieux lui apporter des fleurs que des bonbons**
it would be better to take her flowers than sweets

Note that **il faut** + infinitive is used to state a generality. If one particular person etc is the subject of the action, an indirect object is used:

**il faut réserver à l'avance**
you have to book in advance

**il lui faut se dépêcher**
he has to hurry

iii) verbs of thinking:

**je ne crois pas le connaître**
I don't think I know him

**tu penses être chez toi à cinq heures?**
do you think you'll be home at five?

iv) **pour** and **sans**:

**le car est reparti sans nous attendre**
the coach left without waiting for us

**j'économise pour pouvoir acheter une moto**
I'm saving up to buy a motorbike

## 2. THE CONDITIONAL

**a)** The conditional present

i) The conditional present is used to describe what someone would do or would be doing, or what would happen (if something else were to happen):

**si j'avais de l'argent, je ferais le tour du monde**
if I had money, I would travel around the world

Note that when the main verb is in the conditional present, the verb after **si** is in the imperfect.

ii) It is also used in indirect questions or reported speech instead of the future:

**il ne m'a pas dit s'il *viendrait***
he didn't tell me whether he *would come*

**b)** The conditional perfect (or past conditional)

The conditional perfect or past conditional is used to express what someone would have done or would have been doing or what would have happened:

**si j'avais su, je n'aurais rien dit**
if I had known, I wouldn't have said anything

**qu'aurais-je fait sans toi?**
what would I have done without you?

Note that if the main verb is in the conditional perfect, the verb introduced by **si** is in the pluperfect.

**c)** Tenses after **si**:

The tense of the verb introduced by **si** is determined by the tense of the verb in the main clause:

| MAIN VERB | | VERB FOLLOWING 'SI' |
|---|---|---|
| conditional present | → | imperfect |
| conditional perfect | → | pluperfect |

> je te le dirais si je le savais
> I would tell you if I knew

> je te l'aurais dit si je l'avais su
> I would have told you if I had known

The conditional and the future should never be used with **si** unless **si** means 'whether' (ie when it introduces an indirect question):

> je me demande si j'y serais arrivé sans toi
> I wonder if I would have managed without you

## 3. THE IMPERATIVE

a) *Definition*

The imperative is used to give commands or polite instructions, or to make requests or suggestions; these can be positive ('do!') or negative ('don't!'):

> **mange ta soupe!**
> eat your soup!
>
> **n'aie pas peur!**
> don't be afraid!

> **partons!**
> let's go!
>
> **entrez!**
> come in!

> **faites attention!**
> be careful!
>
> **n'hésitez pas!**
> don't hesitate!

> **tournez à droite à la poste**
> turn right at the post office

b) *Forms*

The imperative has only three forms, which are the same as the **tu**, **nous** and **vous** forms of the present tense, but without the subject pronoun:

|  | -ER VERBS | -IR VERBS | -RE VERBS |
|---|---|---|---|
| 'tu' form: | **regarde**<br>watch | **choisis**<br>choose | **attends**<br>wait |
| 'nous' form: | **regardons**<br>let's watch | **choisissons**<br>let's choose | **attendons**<br>let's wait |

| 'vous' form: | **regardez** | **choisissez** | **attendez** |
|---|---|---|---|
| | watch | choose | wait |

*Note:*

i) The **-s** of the **tu** form of **-er** verbs is dropped, except when **y** or **en** follow the verb:

**parle-lui!**
speak to him!

**parles-en avec lui**
speak to him about it

**achète du sucre!**
buy some sugar!

**achètes-en un kilo**
buy a kilo (of it)

ii) The distinction between the subject pronouns **tu** and **vous** (see p 70) applies to the **tu** and **vous** forms of the imperative:

**prends ta sœur avec toi**
take your sister with you

**prenez le plat du jour, Monsieur; c'est du poulet rôti**
have today's special, sir; it's roast chicken

**ouvrez vos livres à la page 24**
open your books at page 24

c) *Negative commands*

In negative commands, the verb is placed between **ne** and **pas** (or the second part of other negative expressions):

**ne fais pas ça!**
don't do that!

**ne dites rien!**
don't say anything!

d) *Imperative with object pronouns*

In positive commands, object pronouns come after the verb and are attached to it by a hyphen. In negative commands, they come before the verb (see pp 79-85):

**dites-moi ce qui s'est passé**
tell me what happened

**attendons-les!**
let's wait for them

**prends-en bien soin, ne l'abîme pas!**
take good care of it, don't damage it!

**ne le leur dis pas!**
don't tell them (that)!

**ne les écoutez pas**
don't listen to them

**e)** *Imperative of reflexive verbs*

The position of the reflexive pronoun of reflexive verbs is the same as that of object pronouns:

**tais-toi!**
be quiet!

**levez-vous!**
get up!

**méfiez-vous de lui**
don't trust him

**arrêtons-nous ici**
let's stop here

**ne nous plaignons pas**
let's not complain

**ne t'approche pas plus!**
don't come any closer!

**f)** *Alternatives to the imperative*

i) infinitive

the infinitive is often used instead of the imperative in written instructions and in recipes:

**s'adresser au concierge**
see the caretaker

**ne pas fumer**
no smoking

**verser le lait et bien mélanger**
pour in the milk and mix well

ii) subjunctive

as the imperative has no third person (singular or plural), **que** + subjunctive is used for giving orders in the third person:

**que personne ne me dérange!**
don't let anyone disturb me!

**qu'il entre!**
let him (come) in!

**qu'elle parte, je m'en fiche!**
I don't care if she goes!

**g)** *Idiomatic usage*

The imperative is used in spoken French in many set phrases. Here are some of the most common ones:

**allons donc!**
you don't say!
hey! *(protest)*

**dis/dites donc!**
by the way!

**tiens/tenez!**
here you are!

**tiens! voilà le facteur**
ah! here comes the postman

**tiens (donc)!**
(oh) really?

**tiens! tiens!**
well, well!

**voyons!**
come (on) now!

**voyons donc!**
let's see now

## H. The Infinitive

**1.** The infinitive is the basic form of the verb. It is recognizable by its ending, which is found in three forms corresponding to the three conjugations: **-er, -ir, -re**.

These endings give the verb the meaning 'to …':

| | | |
|---|---|---|
| **acheter** | **choisir** | **vendre** |
| to buy | to choose | to sell |

Note that although this applies as a general rule, the French infinitive will often be translated by a verbal construction ending in **-ing** (see pp 256-8).

### 2. Uses of the infinitive

The infinitive can follow a preposition, a verb, a noun, a pronoun, an adverb or an adjective.

a) *After a preposition*

The infinitive can be used after some prepositions (**pour, avant de, sans, au lieu de, afin de** etc):

| | |
|---|---|
| **sans attendre** | **avant de partir** |
| without waiting | before leaving |

b) *After a verb*

There are three main constructions when a verb is followed by an infinitive:

i) Verbs followed by the infinitive with no linking preposition:

❑ verbs of wishing and willing, eg:

| | |
|---|---|
| **vouloir** | to want |
| **souhaiter** | to wish |
| **désirer** | to wish, to want |
| **espérer** | to hope |

**voulez-vous manger maintenant ou plus tard?**
do you want to eat now or later?

**je souhaite parler au directeur**
I wish to speak to the manager

❑ verbs of seeing, hearing and feeling, eg:

| | |
|---|---|
| **voir** | to see |
| **écouter** | to listen to |
| **regarder** | to watch |
| **sentir** | to feel, to smell |
| **entendre** | to hear |

**je l'ai vu jouer**
I've seen him play

**tu m'as regardé danser?**
did you watch me dance?

**j'ai entendu quelqu'un crier**
I heard someone shout

❑ verbs of motion, eg:

| | |
|---|---|
| **aller** | to go |
| **monter** | to go/come up |
| **venir** | to come |
| **entrer** | to go/come in |
| **rentrer** | to go/come home |
| **sortir** | to go/come out |
| **descendre** | to go/come down |

**je viendrai te voir demain**
I'll come and see you tomorrow

**il est descendu laver la voiture**
he went down to wash the car

**va acheter le journal**
go and buy the paper

Note that in English, 'to come' and 'to go' may be linked to the verb that follows by 'and'; 'and' is not translated in French.

**aller** + infinitive can be used to express a future action:

**qu'est-ce que tu vas faire demain?**
what are you going to do tomorrow?

❑ modal auxiliary verbs (see pp 163-6)

□ verbs of liking and disliking, eg:

| | |
|---|---|
| **aimer** | to like |
| **adorer** | to love |
| **aimer mieux** | to prefer |
| **détester** | to hate |
| **préférer** | to prefer |

**tu aimes voyager?**
do you like travelling?

**je déteste aller à la campagne**
I hate going to the country

**j'adore faire la grasse matinée**
I love having a lie-in

**j'aime mieux attendre**
I'd rather wait

□ some impersonal verbs (see p 122)

□ a few other verbs, eg:

| | |
|---|---|
| **compter** | to intend to |
| **sembler** | to seem |
| **laisser** | to let, to allow |
| **faillir** | 'to nearly' (do) |
| **oser** | to dare |

**ils l'ont laissé partir**
they let him go

**je n'ose pas le leur demander**
I daren't ask them

**tu sembles être malade**
you seem to be ill

**je compte partir demain**
I intend to leave tomorrow

**j'ai failli manquer l'avion**
I nearly missed the plane

□ in the following set expressions:

| | |
|---|---|
| **aller chercher** | to go and get, to fetch |
| **envoyer chercher** | to send for |
| **entendre dire (que)** | to hear (that) |

**entendre parler de**      to hear about
**laisser tomber**      to drop
**venir chercher**      to come and get
**vouloir dire**      to mean

**va chercher ton argent**
go and get your money

**j'ai entendu dire qu'il était journaliste**
I've heard that he's a journalist

**tu as entendu parler de ce film?**
have you heard about this film?

**ne le laisse pas tomber!**
don't drop it!

**ça veut dire 'demain'**
it means 'tomorrow'

ii) Verbs followed by **à** + infinitive

A list of these is given on p 201:

**je dois aider ma mère à préparer le déjeuner**
I must help my mother prepare lunch

**il commence à faire nuit**
it's beginning to get dark

**alors, tu t'es décidé à y aller?**
so you've made up your mind to go?

**je t'invite à venir chez moi pour les vacances de Noël**
you are welcome to come to my house for the Christmas holidays

**je passe mon temps à lire et à regarder la télé**
I spend my time reading and watching TV

**cela sert à ouvrir les bouteilles**
this is used for opening bottles

iii) Verbs followed by **de** + infinitive

A list of these is given on pp 202-3:

**je crois qu'il s'est arrêté de pleuvoir**
I think it's stopped raining

**tu as envie de sortir?**
do you feel like going out?

**le médecin a conseillé à Serge de rester au lit**
the doctor advised Serge to stay in bed

**j'ai décidé de rester chez moi**
I decided to stay at home

**essayons de faire du stop**
let's try and hitch-hike

**demande à Papa de t'aider**
ask Dad to help you

**n'oublie pas d'en acheter!**
don't forget to buy some!

**je vous prie de m'excuser**
please forgive me

**tu as fini de m'ennuyer?**
will you stop annoying me?

**je t'interdis d'y aller**
I forbid you to go

**j'ai refusé de le faire**
I refused to do it

**il vient de téléphoner**
he's just phoned

**c)** *After a noun, a pronoun, an adverb or an adjective*

There are two possible constructions:

i) with the linking preposition **à**:

**il avait plusieurs clients à voir**
he had several customers to see

**c'est difficile à dire**
it's difficult to say

**une maison à vendre**
a house for sale

**j'ai des examens à préparer**
I've got exams to prepare

il nous a indiqué la route à suivre
he showed us the road to follow

il n'y a pas de temps à perdre
there's no time to lose

c'était une occasion à ne pas manquer
it was an opportunity not to be missed

❏ **à** conveys the idea of something to do or to be done after the following:

| | |
|---|---|
| beaucoup | a lot |
| plus | more |
| tant | so much |
| trop | too much |
| assez | enough |
| moins | less |
| rien | nothing |
| tout | everything |
| quelque chose | something |

il y a trop de livres à lire
there are too many books to read

il n'y a rien à ajouter
there's nothing further to add

elle a quelque chose à nous annoncer
she has something to tell us

❏ **à** is used in a passive sense (when something is being done) and after **c'est**:

un livre agréable à lire
a pleasant book to read

il est facile à satisfaire
he is easily satisfied

c'est intéressant à savoir
that's interesting to know

c'était impossible à faire
it was impossible to do

ii) with the linking preposition **de**:

**je suis content de te voir**
I am pleased to see you

◻ **de** is used after nouns of an abstract nature, usually with the definite article, eg:

| | |
|---|---|
| **l'habitude de** | the habit of |
| **l'occasion de** | the opportunity to |
| **le temps de** | the time to |
| **le courage de** | the courage to |
| **l'envie de** | the desire to |
| **le besoin de** | the need to |
| **le plaisir de** | the pleasure of |
| **le moment de** | the time to |

**il n'avait pas l'habitude d'être seul**
he wasn't used to being alone

**je n'ai pas le temps de leur expliquer**
I don't have time to explain it to them

**avez-vous eu l'occasion de la rencontrer?**
did you have the opportunity to meet her?

**ce n'est pas le moment de le déranger**
now is not the time to disturb him

**je n'ai pas eu le courage de te le dire**
I didn't have the courage to tell you

◻ **de** is used after **il est** in an impersonal sense (see p 114):

**il est intéressant de savoir que …**
it is interesting to know that …

For information on the use of **c'est** and **il est**, see pp 258-9.

◻ **de** is used after many adjectives, and is frequently used to translate 'of' in English, eg:

| | |
|---|---|
| **certain/sûr de** | certain of/to |
| **capable de** | capable of |
| **incapable de** | incapable of |
| **coupable de** | guilty of |

**j'étais sûr de réussir**
I was sure of succeeding

**il est incapable d'y arriver seul**
he is incapable of managing on his own

□ **de** is also used with adjectives relating to emotions and states of mind, eg:

| | |
|---|---|
| **content de** | pleased/happy to |
| **surpris/étonné de** | surprised to |
| **fier de** | proud to |
| **heureux de** | happy to |
| **fâché de** | annoyed to/at |
| **triste de** | sad to |
| **gêné de** | embarrassed to |
| **désolé de** | sorry for/to |

**j'ai été très content de recevoir ta lettre**
I was very pleased to get your letter

**elle sera surprise de vous voir**
she will be surprised to see you

**nous avons été très tristes d'apprendre la nouvelle**
we were very sad to hear the news

Note, however, that **à** is used with **prêt à** (ready to) and **disposé à** (willing to):

**es-tu prêt à partir?**
are you ready to go?

**je suis tout disposé à vous aider**
I'm very willing to help you

d) *faire* + infinitive

**faire** is followed by an infinitive without any linking preposition to express the sense of 'having someone do something' or 'having something done'; two constructions are possible, depending on whether there are one or two objects:

i) when only one object is used, it is a direct object:

**je dois le faire réparer**
I must have it fixed

**il veut faire repeindre sa voiture**
he wants to have his car resprayed

**cette veste est sale, il faut la faire nettoyer**
this jacket's dirty, I'll have to have it cleaned

**tu m'as fait attendre!**
you kept me waiting!

**je le ferai parler**
I'll make him talk

Note the following set expressions:

**faire entrer**
to show in

**faire venir**
to send for

**faites entrer ce monsieur**
show this gentleman in

**je vais faire venir le docteur**
I'll send for the doctor

ii) when both **faire** and the following infinitive have an object, the
object of **faire** is indirect:

**elle m'a fait prendre une douche**
she made me take a shower

**je leur ai fait ranger leur chambre**
I made them tidy their room

e) *Infinitive used as subject of another verb:*

**trouver un emploi n'est pas facile**
finding a job isn't easy

**devenir pilote était mon rêve**
my dream was to become a pilot

## 3. The perfect infinitive

a) *Form*

The perfect or past infinitive is formed with the infinitive of the
auxiliary **avoir** or **être** as appropriate (see pp 112-17), followed by the
past participle of the verb, eg:

**avoir mangé**
to have eaten

**être allé**
to have gone

**s'être levé**
to have got up

b) *Use*

i) after the preposition **après** (after):

**après avoir attendu une heure, il est rentré chez lui**
after waiting for an hour, he went back home

**j'ai compris la remarque après avoir relu le livre**
I understood the remark after reading the book again

ii) after certain verbs:

| | |
|---|---|
| **se souvenir de** | to remember |
| **remercier de** | to thank for |
| **regretter de** | to regret, to be sorry for |
| **être désolé de** | to be sorry for |

**je vous remercie de m'avoir invité**
thank you for inviting me

**il regrettait de leur avoir menti**
he was sorry he had lied to them

**tu te souviens d'avoir fait cela?**
do you remember doing this?

# I. Participles

## 1. The present participle

a) *Formation*

Like the imperfect, the present participle is formed by using the stem of the first person plural of the present tense (the **nous** form without the **-ons** ending) to which **ant** (like English **ing**) is added. The following three verbs, however, have irregular present participles:

| INFINITIVE | PRESENT PARTICIPLE |
|---|---|
| **avoir** to have | **ayant** having |
| **être** to be | **étant** being |
| **savoir** to know | **sachant** knowing |

b) *Use as an adjective*

Used as an adjective, the present participle agrees in number and in gender with its noun or pronoun:

**un travail fatigant**
tiring work

**la semaine suivante**
the following week

**ils sont très exigeants**
they're very demanding

**des nouvelles surprenantes**
surprising news

c) *Use as a verb*

The present participle is used far less frequently in French than in English, and English present participles in **-ing** are often not translated by a participle in French (see pp 256-8).

i) Used on its own, the present participle corresponds to the English present participle:

**ne voulant plus attendre, ils sont partis sans moi**
not wanting to wait any longer, they left without me

**pensant bien faire, j'ai insisté**
thinking I was doing the right thing, I insisted

ii) **en** + present participle

When the subject of the present participle is the same as that of the main verb, this structure is often used to express simultaneous actions (ie 'while doing something'), manner (ie 'by doing something') and to translate English phrasal verbs expressing motion.

◻ simultaneous actions

In English this structure is translated by:

> while/when/on + present participle (eg 'on arriving')
> while/when/as + subject + verb (eg 'as he arrived')

**il est tombé en descendant l'escalier**
he fell as he was going down the stairs

**en le voyant, j'ai éclaté de rire**
when I saw him, I burst out laughing

**elle lisait le journal en attendant l'autobus**
she was reading the paper while waiting for the bus

Note that the adverb **tout** is often used before **en** to emphasize the fact that the actions are simultaneous, especially when there is an element of contradiction:

**elle écoutait la radio tout en faisant ses devoirs**
she was listening to the radio while doing her homework

**tout en protestant, je les ai suivis**
under protest, I followed them

◻ manner

When expressing how an action is done, **en** + participle is translated by 'by' + participle, eg:

**il gagne sa vie en vendant des voitures d'occasion**
he earns his living (by) selling second-hand cars

**j'ai trouvé du travail en lisant les petites annonces**
I found a job by reading the classified ads

◻ phrasal verbs of motion

**en** + present participle is often used to translate English phrasal verbs expressing motion, where the verb expresses the means of motion and a preposition expresses the direction of movement (eg 'to run out', 'to swim across').

In French, the English preposition is translated by a verb, while the English verb is translated by **en** + present participle.

> **il est sorti du magasin** *en courant*
> he *ran* out of the shop

> **elle a traversé la route** *en titubant*
> she *staggered* across the road

## 2. The past participle

a) *Forms*

For the formation of the past participle see p 112.

b) *Use*

The past participle is mostly used as a verb in compound tenses or in the passive, but it can also be used as an adjective. In either case, there are strict rules of agreement to be followed.

i) When it is used as an adjective, the past participle always agrees with the noun or pronoun to which it refers:

> **un pneu crevé**
> a burst tyre

> **une pomme pourrie**
> a rotten apple

> **ils étaient épuisés**
> they were exhausted

> **des photos prises à la nuit tombée**
> photos taken at nightfall

Note that in French, the past participle is used as an adjective to describe postures or attitudes of the body, where English uses the present participle. The most common of these are:

| | |
|---|---|
| **accoudé** | leaning on one's elbows |
| **accroupi** | squatting |
| **agenouillé** | kneeling |
| **allongé** | lying (down) |
| **appuyé (contre)** | leaning (against) |
| **couché** | lying (down) |
| **étendu** | lying (down) |
| **penché** | leaning (over) |
| **(sus)pendu** | hanging |

**il est allongé sur le lit**
he's lying on the bed

**une femme assise devant moi**
a woman sitting in front of me

ii) In compound tenses:

□ With the auxiliary **avoir** the past participle agrees in number and gender with the direct object only when the direct object comes before the participle, ie in the following cases:

in a clause introduced by the relative pronoun **que**:

**le jeu vidéo que j'ai acheté**      **la valise qu'il a perdue**
the video game I bought               the suitcase he lost

with a direct object pronoun:

**je ne trouve pas la disquette; où l'as-tu mise?**
I can't find the floppy disk; where did you put it?

**merci pour tes suggestions, je les ai trouvées très utiles**
thank you for your suggestions; I found them very useful

in a clause introduced by **combien de, quel** or **lequel**:

**combien de pays as-tu visités?**
how many countries have you visited?

**laquelle avez-vous choisie?**
which one did you choose?

Note that if the direct object comes after the past participle, the participle remains in the masculine singular form:

**on a rencontré des gens très sympathiques**
we met some very nice people

□ With the auxiliary **être** the past participle agrees with the subject of the verb:

**quand est-elle revenue?**      **elle était déjà partie**
when did she come back?          she'd already left

**ils sont passés te voir?**
did they come to see you?

**elles sont restées là**
they stayed here

Note that this rule also applies when the verb is in the passive:

**elle a été arrêtée**
she's been arrested

▫ With reflexive verbs the past participle normally agrees with the reflexive pronoun if the pronoun is a direct object; since the reflexive pronoun refers to the subject, the number and gender of the past participle are determined by the subject:

**Jacques s'est trompé**
Jacques made a mistake

**Marie s'était levée tard**
Marie had got up late

**ils se sont disputés?**
did they have an argument?

**elles se sont vues**
they saw each other

**Michèle et Marie, vous vous êtes habillées?**
Michèle and Marie, have you got dressed yet?

Note, however, that the past participle does not agree when the reflexive pronoun is an indirect object:

**elles se sont écrit**
they wrote *to* each other

**elle s'est lavé les cheveux**
she washed her hair

**ils se sont serré la main**
they shook hands

## J. The Passive

### 1. Formation

The passive is used when the subject does not perform the action, but is subjected to it, eg:

the house has been sold        he was made redundant

Passive tenses are formed with the corresponding tense of the verb **'être'** ('to be', as in English), followed by the past participle of the verb, eg:

**j'ai été invité**
I was invited

The past participle must agree with its subject, eg:

**il sera puni**              **elle a été renvoyée**
he will be punished        she has been dismissed

**ils seront déçus**          **elles ont été vues**
they will be disappointed    they were seen

### 2. Avoidance of the passive

The passive is far less common in French than in English. In particular, an indirect object cannot become the subject of a sentence in French; the following sentence, where 'he' is an indirect object, has no equivalent in French:

he was given a book *(ie a book was given to him)*

In general, French tries to avoid the passive wherever possible. This can be done in several ways.

**a)** *By using the pronoun on:*

**on m'a volé mon portefeuille**
my wallet has been stolen

**on construit une nouvelle piscine**
a new swimming pool is being built

**en France, on boit beaucoup de vin**
a lot of wine is drunk in France

**b)** *By making the agent the subject of the verb*

If the agent, that is the real subject, is mentioned in English, it can become the subject of the French verb:

> **la nouvelle va les surprendre**
> they will be surprised by *the news*

> **mon correspondant m'a invité**
> I've been invited by *my penfriend*

> **mon cadeau te plaît?**
> are you pleased with *my present*?

**c)** *By using a reflexive verb*

Reflexive forms can be created for a large number of verbs, particularly in the third person:

> **elle s'appelle Anne**
> she is called Anne

> **ton absence va se remarquer**
> your absence will be noticed

> **ce plat se mange froid**
> this dish is eaten cold

> **cela ne se fait pas ici**
> that isn't done here

**d)** *By using **se faire** + infinitive (when the subject is a person)*

> **il s'est fait renverser par une voiture**
> he was run over by a car

> **je me suis fait couper les cheveux**
> I've had my hair cut

## 3. Conjugation

For the complete conjugation of a verb in the passive, see **être aimé** (to be loved) p 170.

# K. Modal Auxiliary Verbs

The modal auxiliary verbs are always followed by the infinitive. They express an obligation, a probability, an intention, a possibility or a wish rather than a fact.

The five modal auxiliary verbs are: **devoir, pouvoir, savoir, vouloir,** and **falloir.**

**1. Devoir** (for conjugation see p 178) is used to express the following:

a) *obligation*

> **nous devons arriver à temps**
> we must arrive in time

> **nous avions dû partir**
> we had (had) to go

> **demain tu devras prendre le bus**
> tomorrow you'll have to take the bus

> **j'ai dû avouer que j'avais tort**
> I had to admit that I was wrong

In the conditional, **devoir** may be used for advice, ie to express what should be done (conditional present) or should have been done (conditional past):

> **vous devriez travailler davantage**
> you ought to/should work harder

> **tu ne devrais pas marcher sur l'herbe**
> you shouldn't walk on the grass

> **tu aurais dû tout avouer**
> you should have admitted everything

> **tu n'aurais pas dû manger ces champignons**
> you shouldn't have eaten those mushrooms

Note that the French infinitive is translated by a past participle in English: **man*ger*** = eat*en*.

b) *probability*

> **il doit être en train de dormir**
> he must be sleeping (he's probably sleeping)

163

**j'ai dû me tromper de chemin**
I must have taken the wrong road

Note that in a past narrative sequence in the distant past, 'must have' is translated by a pluperfect in French:

**il dit qu'il avait dû se tromper de chemin**
he said he must have taken the wrong road

c) *intention, expectation*

**je dois aller chez le dentiste**
I am supposed to go to the dentist

**le train doit arriver à 19h30**
the train is due to arrive at 7.30p.m.

**2. Pouvoir** (for conjugation see p 190) is used to express the following:

a) *capacity/ability*

**il peut rester plusieurs jours sans dormir**
he can go without sleep for several days

**cette voiture peut faire du 150**
this car can go up to 93 mph

**il était si faible qu'il ne pouvait pas sortir de son lit**
he was so weak that he couldn't get out of bed

b) *permission*

| | |
|---|---|
| **puis-je entrer?** | **puis-je vous offrir du thé?** |
| may I come in? | may I offer you some tea? |

c) *possibility*

| | |
|---|---|
| **cela peut arriver** | **ça peut n'avoir aucune importance** |
| it can happen | it might not be at all important |

Note that **pouvoir** + the infinitive is usually replaced by **peut-être** + the finite tense, eg **il s'est peut-être trompé de livres** (he may have taken the wrong books).

In the conditional, **pouvoir** is used to express something that could or might be (conditional present) or that could or might have been (conditional past):

> **tu pourrais t'excuser**
> you might apologize

> **j'aurais pu vous prêter mon téléphone portable**
> I could have lent you my mobile phone

Note that with verbs of perception, eg **entendre** (to hear), **sentir** (to feel, to smell), **voir** (to see), **pouvoir** is often omitted.

> **j'entendais le bruit des vagues**
> I could hear the sound of the waves

**3. Savoir** (for conjugation see p 193) is used to express 'to know how to':

> **je sais/savais conduire une moto**
> I can/used to be able to ride a motorbike

> **elle sait parler plusieurs langues**
> she can speak several languages

**4. Vouloir** (for conjugation see p 199) is used to express the following:

**a)** *desire*

> **je veux partir**
> I want to go

> **voulez-vous danser avec moi?**
> will you dance with me?

**b)** *wish*

> **je voudrais être riche**
> I wish I were rich

> **je voudrais trouver un travail intéressant**
> I'd like to find an interesting job

> **j'aurais voulu te donner un coup de poing**
> I would have liked to punch you

**c)** *intention*

> **il a voulu sauter par la fenêtre**
> he tried to jump out of the window

Note that **veuillez**, the imperative of **vouloir**, is used as a polite form to express a request ('would you please …'):

**veuillez ne pas déranger**
please do not disturb

**5. Falloir** (for conjugation see p 185) is used to express necessity:

**il faut manger pour vivre**
you must eat to live

**il faudrait y aller tout de suite**
we should go right away

**il aurait fallu apporter des sandwichs**
we should have brought sandwiches

Note that some of the above verbs can also be used without infinitive constructions in which case they have a different meaning, eg **devoir** = to owe, **savoir** = to know.

**je te dois 20 euros**
I owe you 20 euros

**elle le sait par cœur**
she knows it by heart

# L. Conjugation Tables

The following verbs provide the main patterns of conjugation including the conjugation of the most common irregular verbs. They are arranged in alphabetical order:

| | |
|---|---|
| **-er** verb *(see p 100)* | AIMER |
| **-ir** verb *(see p 100)* | FINIR |
| **-re** verb *(see p 100)* | VENDRE |
| Reflexive verb *(see pp 118-21)* | SE MÉFIER |
| Verb with auxiliary **être** *(see pp 114-7)* | ARRIVER |
| Verb in the passive *(see pp 161-2)* | ÊTRE AIMÉ |
| Auxiliaries *(see pp 112-7)* | AVOIR |
| | ÊTRE |
| | |
| Verb in **-eler/-eter** *(see pp 106-7)* | APPELER |
| Verb in **-e** + consonant + **er** *(see pp 109)* | ACHETER |
| Verb in **é** + consonant + **er** *(see pp 110-11)* | ESPÉRER |
| Modal auxiliaries *(see pp 163-6)* | DEVOIR |
| | POUVOIR |
| | SAVOIR |
| | VOULOIR |
| | FALLOIR |

| | | |
|---|---|---|
| Irregular verbs | ALLER | METTRE |
| | CONDUIRE | OUVRIR |
| | CONNAÎTRE | PRENDRE |
| | CROIRE | RECEVOIR |
| | DIRE | TENIR |
| | DORMIR | VENIR |
| | ÉCRIRE | VIVRE |
| | FAIRE | VOIR |

'**Harrap French Verbs**', a fully comprehensive list of French verbs and their conjugations, is also available in this series.

# VERBS

## ACHETER    to buy

| PRESENT | IMPERFECT | FUTURE |
|---|---|---|
| j'achète | j'achetais | j'achèterai |
| tu achètes | tu achetais | tu achèteras |
| il achète | il achetait | il achètera |
| nous achetons | nous achetions | nous achèterons |
| vous achetez | vous achetiez | vous achèterez |
| ils achètent | ils achetaient | ils achèteront |

| PAST HISTORIC | PERFECT | PLUPERFECT |
|---|---|---|
| j'achetai | j'ai acheté | j'avais acheté |
| tu achetas | tu as acheté | tu avais acheté |
| il acheta | il a acheté | il avait acheté |
| nous achetâmes | nous avons acheté | nous avions acheté |
| vous achetâtes | vous avez acheté | vous aviez acheté |
| ils achetèrent | ils ont acheté | ils avaient acheté |

### CONDITIONAL

| PAST ANTERIOR | PRESENT | PAST |
|---|---|---|
| j'eus acheté etc | j'achèterais | j'aurais acheté |
|  | tu achèterais | tu aurais acheté |
|  | il achèterait | il aurait acheté |
|  | nous achèterions | nous aurions acheté |
| FUTURE PERFECT | vous achèteriez | vous auriez acheté |
| j'aurai acheté etc | ils achèteraient | ils auraient acheté |

### SUBJUNCTIVE

| PRESENT | IMPERFECT | PERFECT |
|---|---|---|
| j'achète | j'achetasse | j'aie acheté |
| tu achètes | tu achetasses | tu aies acheté |
| il achète | il achetât | il ait acheté |
| nous achetions | nous achetassions | nous ayons acheté |
| vous achetiez | vous achetassiez | vous ayez acheté |
| ils achètent | ils achetassent | ils aient acheté |

| IMPERATIVE | INFINITIVE | PARTICIPLE |
|---|---|---|
| achète | **PRESENT** | **PRESENT** |
| achetons | acheter | achetant |
| achetez |  |  |
|  | **PAST** | **PAST** |
|  | avoir acheté | acheté |

# AIMER

to like/to love

| PRESENT | IMPERFECT | FUTURE |
|---|---|---|
| j'aime | j'aimais | j'aimerai |
| tu aimes | tu aimais | tu aimeras |
| il aime | il aimait | il aimera |
| nous aimons | nous aimions | nous aimerons |
| vous aimez | vous aimiez | vous aimerez |
| ils aiment | ils aimaient | ils aimeront |

| PAST HISTORIC | PERFECT | PLUPERFECT |
|---|---|---|
| j'aimai | j'ai aimé | j'avais aimé |
| tu aimas | tu as aimé | tu avais aimé |
| il aima | il a aimé | il avait aimé |
| nous aimâmes | nous avons aimé | nous avions aimé |
| vous aimâtes | vous avez aimé | vous aviez aimé |
| ils aimèrent | ils ont aimé | ils avaient aimé |

## CONDITIONAL

| PAST ANTERIOR | PRESENT | PAST |
|---|---|---|
| j'eus aimé etc | j'aimerais | j'aurais aimé |
| | tu aimerais | tu aurais aimé |
| | il aimerait | il aurait aimé |
| | nous aimerions | nous aurions aimé |
| FUTURE PERFECT | vous aimeriez | vous auriez aimé |
| j'aurai aimé etc | ils aimeraient | ils auraient aimé |

## SUBJUNCTIVE

| PRESENT | IMPERFECT | PERFECT |
|---|---|---|
| j'aime | j'aimasse | j'aie aimé |
| tu aimes | tu aimasses | tu aies aimé |
| il aime | il aimât | il ait aimé |
| nous aimions | nous aimassions | nous ayons aimé |
| vous aimiez | vous aimassiez | vous ayez aimé |
| ils aiment | ils aimassent | ils aient aimé |

| IMPERATIVE | INFINITIVE | PARTICIPLE |
|---|---|---|
| aime | PRESENT | PRESENT |
| aimons | aimer | aimant |
| aimez | | |
| | PAST | PAST |
| | avoir aimé | aimé |

## ÊTRE AIMÉ  to be loved

| PRESENT | IMPERFECT | FUTURE |
|---|---|---|
| je suis aimé(e) | j'étais aimé(e) | je serai aimé(e) |
| tu es aimé(e) | tu étais aimé(e) | tu seras aimé(e) |
| il (elle) est aimé(e) | il (elle) était aimé(e) | il (elle) sera aimé(e) |
| nous sommes aimé(e)s | nous étions aimé(e)s | nous serons aimé(e)s |
| vous êtes aimé(e)(s) | vous étiez aimé(e)(s) | vous serez aimé(e)(s) |
| ils (elles) sont aimé(e)s | ils (elles) étaient aimé(e)s | ils seront aimé(e)s |

| PAST HISTORIC | PERFECT | PLUPERFECT |
|---|---|---|
| je fus aimé(e) | j'ai été aimé(e) | j'avais été aimé(e) |
| tu fus aimé(e) | tu as été aimé(e) | tu avais été aimé(e) |
| il (elle) fut aimé(e) | il (elle) a été aimé(e) | il (elle) avait été aimé(e) |
| nous fûmes aimé(e)s | nous avons été aimé(e)s | nous avions été aimé(e)s |
| vous fûtes aimé(e)(s) | vous avez été aimé(e)(s) | vous aviez été aimé(e)(s) |
| ils (elles) furent aimé(e)s | ils (elles) ont été aimé(e)s | ils (elles) avaient été aimé(e)s |

### CONDITIONAL

| PAST ANTERIOR | PRESENT | PAST |
|---|---|---|
| j'eus été aimé(e) etc | je serais aimé(e) | j'aurais été aimé(e) |
| | tu serais aimé(e) | tu aurais été aimé(e) |
| | il (elle) serait aimé(e) | il (elle) aurait été aimé(e) |
| | nous serions aimé(e)s | nous aurions été aimé(e)s |
| **FUTURE PERFECT** | vous seriez aimé(e)(s) | vous auriez été aimé(e)(s) |
| j'aurai été aimé(e) etc | ils (elles) seraient aimé(e)s | ils (elles) auraient été aimé(e)s |

### SUBJUNCTIVE

| PRESENT | IMPERFECT | PERFECT |
|---|---|---|
| je sois aimé(e) | je fusse aimé(e) | j'aie été aimé(e) |
| tu sois aimé(e) | tu fusses aimé(e) | tu aies été aimé(e) |
| il (elle) soit aimé(e) | il (elle) fût aimé(e) | il (elle) ait été aimé(e) |
| nous soyons aimé(e)s | nous fussions aimé(e)s | nous ayons été aimé(e)s |
| vous soyez aimé(e)(s) | vous fussiez aimé(e)(s) | vous ayez été aimé(e)(s) |
| ils (elles) soient aimé(e)s | ils (elles) fussent aimé(e)s | ils (elles) aient été aimé(e)s |

| IMPERATIVE | INFINITIVE | PARTICIPLE |
|---|---|---|
| sois aimé(e) | **PRESENT** | **PRESENT** |
| soyons aimé(e)s | être aimé(e)(s) | étant aimé(e)(s) |
| soyez aimé(e)(s) | | |
| | **PAST** | **PAST** |
| | avoir été aimé(e)(s) | été aimé(e)(s) |

# ALLER    to go

| PRESENT | IMPERFECT | FUTURE |
|---|---|---|
| je vais | j'allais | j'irai |
| tu vas | tu allais | tu iras |
| il va | il allait | il ira |
| nous allons | nous allions | nous irons |
| vous allez | vous alliez | vous irez |
| ils vont | ils allaient | ils iront |

| PAST HISTORIC | PERFECT | PLUPERFECT |
|---|---|---|
| j'allai | je suis allé(e) | j'étais allé(e) |
| tu allas | tu es allé(e) | tu étais allé(e) |
| il alla | il (elle) est allé(e) | il (elle) était allé(e) |
| nous allâmes | nous sommes allé(e)s | nous étions allé(e)s |
| vous allâtes | vous êtes allé(e)(s) | vous étiez allé(e)(s) |
| ils allèrent | ils (elles) sont allé(e)s | ils (elles) étaient allé(e)s |

## CONDITIONAL

| PAST ANTERIOR | PRESENT | PAST |
|---|---|---|
| je fus allé(e) etc | j'irais | je serais allé(e) |
| | tu irais | tu serais allé(e) |
| | il irait | il (elle) serait allé(e) |
| | nous irions | nous serions allé(e)s |
| FUTURE PERFECT | vous iriez | vous seriez allé(e)(s) |
| je serai allé(e) etc | ils iraient | ils (elles) seraient allé(e)s |

## SUBJUNCTIVE

| PRESENT | IMPERFECT | PERFECT |
|---|---|---|
| j'aille | j'allasse | je sois allé(e) |
| tu ailles | tu allasses | tu sois allé(e) |
| il aille | il allât | il (elle) soit allé(e) |
| nous allions | nous allassions | nous soyons allé(e)s |
| vous alliez | vous allassiez | vous soyez allé(e)(s) |
| ils aillent | ils allassent | ils (elles) soient allé(e)s |

| IMPERATIVE | INFINITIVE | PARTICIPLE |
|---|---|---|
| va | PRESENT | PRESENT |
| allons | aller | allant |
| allez | | |
| | PAST | PAST |
| | être allé(e)(s) | allé |

## **APPELER**   to call

| PRESENT | IMPERFECT | FUTURE |
|---|---|---|
| j'appelle | j'appelais | j'appellerai |
| tu appelles | tu appelais | tu appelleras |
| il appelle | il appelait | il appellera |
| nous appelons | nous appelions | nous appellerons |
| vous appelez | vous appeliez | vous appellerez |
| ils appellent | ils appelaient | ils appelleront |

| PAST HISTORIC | PERFECT | PLUPERFECT |
|---|---|---|
| j'appelai | j'ai appelé | j'avais appelé |
| tu appelas | tu as appelé | tu avais appelé |
| il appela | il a appelé | il avait appelé |
| nous appelâmes | nous avons appelé | nous avions appelé |
| vous appelâtes | vous avez appelé | vous aviez appelé |
| ils appelèrent | ils ont appelé | ils avaient appelé |

### CONDITIONAL

| PAST ANTERIOR | PRESENT | PAST |
|---|---|---|
| j'eus appelé etc | j'appellerais | j'aurais appelé |
| | tu appellerais | tu aurais appelé |
| | il appellerait | il aurait appelé |
| | nous appellerions | nous aurions appelé |
| **FUTURE PERFECT** | vous appelleriez | vous auriez appelé |
| j'aurai appelé etc | ils appelleraient | ils auraient appelé |

### SUBJUNCTIVE

| PRESENT | IMPERFECT | PERFECT |
|---|---|---|
| j'appelle | j'appelasse | j'aie appelé |
| tu appelles | tu appelasses | tu aies appelé |
| il appelle | il appelât | il ait appelé |
| nous appelions | nous appelassions | nous ayons appelé |
| vous appeliez | vous appelassiez | vous ayez appelé |
| ils appellent | ils appelassent | ils aient appelé |

| IMPERATIVE | INFINITIVE | PARTICIPLE |
|---|---|---|
| appelle | **PRESENT** | **PRESENT** |
| appelons | appeler | appelant |
| appelez | | |
| | **PAST** | **PAST** |
| | avoir appelé | appelé |

# **ARRIVER**   to arrive/to happen

## PRESENT
j'arrive
tu arrives
il arrive
nous arrivons
vous arrivez
ils arrivent

## PAST HISTORIC
j'arrivai
tu arrivas
il arriva
nous arrivâmes
vous arrivâtes
ils arrivèrent

## IMPERFECT
j'arrivais
tu arrivais
il arrivait
nous arrivions
vous arriviez
ils arrivaient

## PERFECT
je suis arrivé(e)
tu es arrivé(e)
il (elle) est arrivé(e)
nous sommes arrivé(e)s
vous êtes arrivé(e)(s)
ils (elles) sont arrivé(e)s

## FUTURE
j'arriverai
tu arriveras
il arrivera
nous arriverons
vous arriverez
ils arriveront

## PLUPERFECT
j'étais arrivé(e)
tu étais arrivé(e)
il (elle) était arrivé(e)
nous étions arrivé(e)s
vous étiez arrivé(e)(s)
ils (elles) étaient arrivé(e)s

## CONDITIONAL

## PAST ANTERIOR
je fus arrivé(e) etc

## FUTURE PERFECT
je serai arrivé(e) etc

## PRESENT
j'arriverais
tu arriverais
il arriverait
nous arriverions
vous arriveriez
ils arriveraient

## PAST
je serais arrivé(e)
tu serais arrivé(e)
il (elle) serait arrivé(e)
nous serions arrivé(e)s
vous seriez arrivé(e)(s)
ils (elles) seraient arrivé(e)s

## SUBJUNCTIVE

## PRESENT
j'arrive
tu arrives
il arrive
nous arrivions
vous arriviez
ils arrivent

## IMPERFECT
j'arrivasse
tu arrivasses
il arrivât
nous arrivassions
vous arrivassiez
ils arrivassent

## PERFECT
je sois arrivé(e)
tu sois arrivé(e)
il (elle) soit arrivé(e)
nous soyons arrivé(e)s
vous soyez arrivé(e)(s)
ils (elles) soient arrivé(e)s

## IMPERATIVE
arrive
arrivons
arrivez

## INFINITIVE
### PRESENT
arriver

### PAST
être arrivé(e)(s)

## PARTICIPLE
### PRESENT
arrivant

### PAST
arrivé

# AVOIR    to have

| PRESENT | IMPERFECT | FUTURE |
|---|---|---|
| j'ai | j'avais | j'aurai |
| tu as | tu avais | tu auras |
| il a | il avait | il aura |
| nous avons | nous avions | nous aurons |
| vous avez | vous aviez | vous aurez |
| ils ont | ils avaient | ils auront |

| PAST HISTORIC | PERFECT | PLUPERFECT |
|---|---|---|
| j'eus | j'ai eu | j'avais eu |
| tu eus | tu as eu | tu avais eu |
| il eut | il a eu | il avait eu |
| nous eûmes | nous avons eu | nous avions eu |
| vous eûtes | vous avez eu | vous aviez eu |
| ils eurent | ils ont eu | ils avaient eu |

## CONDITIONAL

| PAST ANTERIOR | PRESENT | PAST |
|---|---|---|
| j'eus eu etc | j'aurais | j'aurais eu |
| | tu aurais | tu aurais eu |
| | il aurait | il aurait eu |
| | nous aurions | nous aurions eu |
| **FUTURE PERFECT** | vous auriez | vous auriez eu |
| j'aurai eu etc | ils auraient | ils auraient eu |

## SUBJUNCTIVE

| PRESENT | IMPERFECT | PERFECT |
|---|---|---|
| j'aie | j'eusse | j'aie eu |
| tu aies | tu eusses | tu aies eu |
| il ait | il eût | il ait eu |
| nous ayons | nous eussions | nous ayons eu |
| vous ayez | vous eussiez | vous ayez eu |
| ils aient | ils eussent | ils aient eu |

| IMPERATIVE | INFINITIVE | PARTICIPLE |
|---|---|---|
| | PRESENT | PRESENT |
| aie | avoir | ayant |
| ayons | | |
| ayez | | |
| | PAST | PAST |
| | avoir eu | eu |

# **CONDUIRE**  to lead/to drive

| PRESENT | IMPERFECT | FUTURE |
|---|---|---|
| je conduis | je conduisais | je conduirai |
| tu conduis | tu conduisais | tu conduiras |
| il conduit | il conduisait | il conduira |
| nous conduisons | nous conduisions | nous conduirons |
| vous conduisez | vous conduisiez | vous conduirez |
| ils conduisent | ils conduisaient | ils conduiront |

| PAST HISTORIC | PERFECT | PLUPERFECT |
|---|---|---|
| je conduisis | j'ai conduit | j'avais conduit |
| tu conduisis | tu as conduit | tu avais conduit |
| il conduisit | il a conduit | il avait conduit |
| nous conduisîmes | nous avons conduit | nous avions conduit |
| vous conduisîtes | vous avez conduit | vous aviez conduit |
| ils conduisirent | ils ont conduit | ils avaient conduit |

## CONDITIONAL

| PAST ANTERIOR | PRESENT | PAST |
|---|---|---|
| j'eus conduit etc | je conduirais | j'aurais conduit |
| | tu conduirais | tu aurais conduit |
| | il conduirait | il aurait conduit |
| | nous conduirions | nous aurions conduit |
| FUTURE PERFECT | vous conduiriez | vous auriez conduit |
| j'aurai conduit etc | ils conduiraient | ils auraient conduit |

## SUBJUNCTIVE

| PRESENT | IMPERFECT | PERFECT |
|---|---|---|
| je conduise | je conduisisse | j'aie conduit |
| tu conduises | tu conduisisses | tu aies conduit |
| il conduise | il conduisît | il ait conduit |
| nous conduisions | nous conduisissions | nous ayons conduit |
| vous conduisiez | vous conduisissiez | vous ayez conduit |
| ils conduisent | ils conduisissent | ils aient conduit |

| IMPERATIVE | INFINITIVE | PARTICIPLE |
|---|---|---|
| conduis | PRESENT | PRESENT |
| conduisons | conduire | conduisant |
| conduisez | | |
| | PAST | PAST |
| | avoir conduit | conduit |

175

# **CONNAÎTRE** to know

| PRESENT | IMPERFECT | FUTURE |
|---|---|---|
| je connais | je connaissais | je connaîtrai |
| tu connais | tu connaissais | tu connaîtras |
| il connaît | il connaissait | il connaîtra |
| nous connaissons | nous connaissions | nous connaîtrons |
| vous connaissez | vous connaissiez | vous connaîtrez |
| ils connaissent | ils connaissaient | ils connaîtront |

| PAST HISTORIC | PERFECT | PLUPERFECT |
|---|---|---|
| je connus | j'ai connu | j'avais connu |
| tu connus | tu as connu | tu avais connu |
| il connut | il a connu | il avait connu |
| nous connûmes | nous avons connu | nous avions connu |
| vous connûtes | vous avez connu | vous aviez connu |
| ils connurent | ils ont connu | ils avaient connu |

## CONDITIONAL

| PAST ANTERIOR | PRESENT | PAST |
|---|---|---|
| j'eus connu etc | je connaîtrais | j'aurais connu |
| | tu connaîtrais | tu aurais connu |
| | il connaîtrait | il aurait connu |
| | nous connaîtrions | nous aurions connu |
| FUTURE PERFECT | vous connaîtriez | vous auriez connu |
| j'aurai connu etc | ils connaîtraient | ils auraient connu |

## SUBJUNCTIVE

| PRESENT | IMPERFECT | PERFECT |
|---|---|---|
| je connaisse | je connusse | j'aie connu |
| tu connaisses | tu connusses | tu aies connu |
| il connaisse | il connût | il ait connu |
| nous connaissions | nous connussions | nous ayons connu |
| vous connaissiez | vous connussiez | vous ayez connu |
| ils connaissent | ils connussent | ils aient connu |

| IMPERATIVE | INFINITIVE | PARTICIPLE |
|---|---|---|
| connais | **PRESENT** | **PRESENT** |
| connaissons | connaître | connaissant |
| connaissez | | |
| | **PAST** | **PAST** |
| | avoir connu | connu |

# CROIRE    to believe

| PRESENT | IMPERFECT | FUTURE |
|---|---|---|
| je crois | je croyais | je croirai |
| tu crois | tu croyais | tu croiras |
| il croit | il croyait | il croira |
| nous croyons | nous croyions | nous croirons |
| vous croyez | vous croyiez | vous croirez |
| ils croient | ils croyaient | ils croiront |

| PAST HISTORIC | PERFECT | PLUPERFECT |
|---|---|---|
| je crus | j'ai cru | j'avais cru |
| tu crus | tu as cru | tu avais cru |
| il crut | il a cru | il avait cru |
| nous crûmes | nous avons cru | nous avions cru |
| vous crûtes | vous avez cru | vous aviez cru |
| ils crurent | ils ont cru | ils avaient cru |

## CONDITIONAL

| PAST ANTERIOR | PRESENT | PAST |
|---|---|---|
| j'eus cru etc | je croirais | j'aurais cru |
| | tu croirais | tu aurais cru |
| | il croirait | il aurait cru |
| | nous croirions | nous aurions cru |
| FUTURE PERFECT | vous croiriez | vous auriez cru |
| j'aurai cru etc | ils croiraient | ils auraient cru |

## SUBJUNCTIVE

| PRESENT | IMPERFECT | PERFECT |
|---|---|---|
| je croie | je crusse | j'aie cru |
| tu croies | tu crusses | tu aies cru |
| il croie | il crût | il ait cru |
| nous croyions | nous crussions | nous ayons cru |
| vous croyiez | vous crussiez | vous ayez cru |
| ils croient | ils crussent | ils aient cru |

| IMPERATIVE | INFINITIVE | PARTICIPLE |
|---|---|---|
| crois | **PRESENT** | **PRESENT** |
| croyons | croire | croyant |
| croyez | | |
| | **PAST** | **PAST** |
| | avoir cru | cru |

# DEVOIR to owe/to have to

| PRESENT | IMPERFECT | FUTURE |
|---|---|---|
| je dois | je devais | je devrai |
| tu dois | tu devais | tu devras |
| il doit | il devait | il devra |
| nous devons | nous devions | nous devrons |
| vous devez | vous deviez | vous devrez |
| ils doivent | ils devaient | ils devront |

| PAST HISTORIC | PERFECT | PLUPERFECT |
|---|---|---|
| je dus | j'ai dû | j'avais dû |
| tu dus | tu as dû | tu avais dû |
| il dut | il a dû | il avait dû |
| nous dûmes | nous avons dû | nous avions dû |
| vous dûtes | vous avez dû | vous aviez dû |
| ils durent | ils ont dû | ils avaient dû |

## CONDITIONAL

| PAST ANTERIOR | PRESENT | PAST |
|---|---|---|
| j'eus dû etc | je devrais | j'aurais dû |
| | tu devrais | tu aurais dû |
| | il devrait | il aurait dû |
| | nous devrions | nous aurions dû |
| FUTURE PERFECT | vous devriez | vous auriez dû |
| j'aurai dû | ils devraient | ils auraient dû |

## SUBJUNCTIVE

| PRESENT | IMPERFECT | PERFECT |
|---|---|---|
| je doive | je dusse | j'aie dû |
| tu doives | tu dusses | tu aies dû |
| il doive | il dût | il ait dû |
| nous devions | nous dussions | nous ayons dû |
| vous deviez | vous dussiez | vous ayez dû |
| ils doivent | ils dussent | ils aient dû |

| IMPERATIVE | INFINITIVE | PARTICIPLE |
|---|---|---|
| dois | PRESENT | PRESENT |
| devons | devoir | devant |
| devez | | |
| | PAST | PAST |
| | avoir dû | dû (due, dus) |

# DIRE

to say

| PRESENT | IMPERFECT | FUTURE |
|---------|-----------|--------|
| je dis | je disais | je dirai |
| tu dis | tu disais | tu diras |
| il dit | il disait | il dira |
| nous disons | nous disions | nous dirons |
| vous dites | vous disiez | vous direz |
| ils disent | ils disaient | ils diront |

| PAST HISTORIC | PERFECT | PLUPERFECT |
|---------------|---------|------------|
| je dis | j'ai dit | j'avais dit |
| tu dis | tu as dit | tu avais dit |
| il dit | il a dit | il avait dit |
| nous dîmes | nous avons dit | nous avions dit |
| vous dîtes | vous avez dit | vous aviez dit |
| ils dirent | ils ont dit | ils avaient dit |

## CONDITIONAL

| PAST ANTERIOR | PRESENT | PAST |
|---------------|---------|------|
| j'eus dit etc | je dirais | j'aurais dit |
| | tu dirais | tu aurais dit |
| | il dirait | il aurait dit |
| | nous dirions | nous aurions dit |
| FUTURE PERFECT | vous diriez | vous auriez dit |
| j'aurai dit etc | ils diraient | ils auraient dit |

## SUBJUNCTIVE

| PRESENT | IMPERFECT | PERFECT |
|---------|-----------|---------|
| je dise | je disse | j'aie dit |
| tu dises | tu disses | tu aies dit |
| il dise | il dît | il ait dit |
| nous disions | nous dissions | nous ayons dit |
| vous disiez | vous dissiez | vous ayez dit |
| ils disent | ils dissent | ils aient dit |

| IMPERATIVE | INFINITIVE | PARTICIPLE |
|------------|------------|------------|
| dis | **PRESENT** | **PRESENT** |
| disons | dire | disant |
| dites | | |
| | **PAST** | **PAST** |
| | avoir dit | dit |

## DORMIR    to sleep

| PRESENT | IMPERFECT | FUTURE |
|---|---|---|
| je dors | je dormais | je dormirai |
| tu dors | tu dormais | tu dormiras |
| il dort | il dormait | il dormira |
| nous dormons | nous dormions | nous dormirons |
| vous dormez | vous dormiez | vous dormirez |
| ils dorment | ils dormaient | ils dormiront |

| PAST HISTORIC | PERFECT | PLUPERFECT |
|---|---|---|
| je dormis | j'ai dormi | j'avais dormi |
| tu dormis | tu as dormi | tu avais dormi |
| il dormit | il a dormi | il avait dormi |
| nous dormîmes | nous avons dormi | nous avions dormi |
| vous dormîtes | vous avez dormi | vous aviez dormi |
| ils dormirent | ils ont dormi | ils avaient dormi |

### CONDITIONAL

| PAST ANTERIOR | PRESENT | PAST |
|---|---|---|
| j'eus dormi etc | je dormirais | j'aurais dormi |
| | tu dormirais | tu aurais dormi |
| | il dormirait | il aurait dormi |
| | nous dormirions | nous aurions dormi |
| **FUTURE PERFECT** | vous dormiriez | vous auriez dormi |
| j'aurai dormi etc | ils dormiraient | ils auraient dormi |

### SUBJUNCTIVE

| PRESENT | IMPERFECT | PERFECT |
|---|---|---|
| je dorme | je dormisse | j'aie dormi |
| tu dormes | tu dormisses | tu aies dormi |
| il dorme | il dormît | il ait dormi |
| nous dormions | nous dormissions | nous ayons dormi |
| vous dormiez | vous dormissiez | vous ayez dormi |
| ils dorment | ils dormissent | ils aient dormi |

| IMPERATIVE | INFINITIVE | PARTICIPLE |
|---|---|---|
| dors | **PRESENT** | **PRESENT** |
| dormons | dormir | dormant |
| dormez | | |
| | **PAST** | **PAST** |
| | avoir dormi | dormi |

# ÉCRIRE     to write

| PRESENT | IMPERFECT | FUTURE |
|---|---|---|
| j'écris | j'écrivais | j'écrirai |
| tu écris | tu écrivais | tu écriras |
| il écrit | il écrivait | il écrira |
| nous écrivons | nous écrivions | nous écrirons |
| vous écrivez | vous écriviez | vous écrirez |
| ils écrivent | ils écrivaient | ils écriront |

| PAST HISTORIC | PERFECT | PLUPERFECT |
|---|---|---|
| j'écrivis | j'ai écrit | j'avais écrit |
| tu écrivis | tu as écrit | tu avais écrit |
| il écrivit | il a écrit | il avait écrit |
| nous écrivîmes | nous avons écrit | nous avions écrit |
| vous écrivîtes | vous avez écrit | vous aviez écrit |
| ils écrivirent | ils ont écrit | ils avaient écrit |

## CONDITIONAL

| PAST ANTERIOR | PRESENT | PAST |
|---|---|---|
| j'eus écrit etc | j'écrirais | j'aurais écrit |
| | tu écrirais | tu aurais écrit |
| | il écrirait | il aurait écrit |
| | nous écririons | nous aurions écrit |
| FUTURE PERFECT | vous écririez | vous auriez écrit |
| j'aurai écrit etc | ils écriraient | ils auraient écrit |

## SUBJUNCTIVE

| PRESENT | IMPERFECT | PERFECT |
|---|---|---|
| j'écrive | j'écrivisse | j'aie écrit |
| tu écrives | tu écrivisses | tu aies écrit |
| il écrive | il écrivît | il ait écrit |
| nous écrivions | nous écrivissions | nous ayons écrit |
| vous écriviez | vous écrivissiez | vous ayez écrit |
| ils écrivent | ils écrivissent | ils aient écrit |

| IMPERATIVE | INFINITIVE | PARTICIPLE |
|---|---|---|
| écris | PRESENT | PRESENT |
| écrivons | écrire | écrivant |
| écrivez | | |
| | PAST | PAST |
| | avoir écrit | écrit |

# VERBS

## ESPÉRER  to hope

| PRESENT | IMPERFECT | FUTURE |
|---|---|---|
| j'espère | j'espérais | j'espérerai |
| tu espères | tu espérais | tu espéreras |
| il espère | il espérait | il espérera |
| nous espérons | nous espérions | nous espérerons |
| vous espérez | vous espériez | vous espérerez |
| ils espèrent | ils espéraient | ils espéreront |

| PAST HISTORIC | PERFECT | PLUPERFECT |
|---|---|---|
| j'espérai | j'ai espéré | j'avais espéré |
| tu espéras | tu as espéré | tu avais espéré |
| il espéra | il a espéré | il avait espéré |
| nous espérâmes | nous avons espéré | nous avions espéré |
| vous espérâtes | vous avez espéré | vous aviez espéré |
| ils espérèrent | ils ont espéré | ils avaient espéré |

### CONDITIONAL

| PAST ANTERIOR | PRESENT | PAST |
|---|---|---|
| j'eus espéré etc | j'espérerais | j'aurais espéré |
| | tu espérerais | tu aurais espéré |
| | il espérerait | il aurait espéré |
| | nous espérerions | nous aurions espéré |
| FUTURE PERFECT | vous espéreriez | vous auriez espéré |
| j'aurai espéré etc | ils espéreraient | ils auraient espéré |

### SUBJUNCTIVE

| PRESENT | IMPERFECT | PERFECT |
|---|---|---|
| j'espère | j'espérasse | j'aie espéré |
| tu espères | tu espérasses | tu aies espéré |
| il espère | il espérât | il ait espéré |
| nous espérions | nous espérassions | nous ayons espéré |
| vous espériez | vous espérassiez | vous ayez espéré |
| ils espèrent | ils espérassent | ils aient espéré |

| IMPERATIVE | INFINITIVE | PARTICIPLE |
|---|---|---|
| espère | **PRESENT** | **PRESENT** |
| espérons | espérer | espérant |
| espérez | | |
| | **PAST** | **PAST** |
| | avoir espéré | espéré |

# ÊTRE    to be

| PRESENT | IMPERFECT | FUTURE |
|---|---|---|
| je suis | j'étais | je serai |
| tu es | tu étais | tu seras |
| il est | il était | il sera |
| nous sommes | nous étions | nous serons |
| vous êtes | vous étiez | vous serez |
| ils sont | ils étaient | ils seront |

| PAST HISTORIC | PERFECT | PLUPERFECT |
|---|---|---|
| je fus | j'ai été | j'avais été |
| tu fus | tu as été | tu avais été |
| il fut | il a été | il avait été |
| nous fûmes | nous avons été | nous avions été |
| vous fûtes | vous avez été | vous aviez été |
| ils furent | ils ont été | ils avaient été |

## CONDITIONAL

| PAST ANTERIOR | PRESENT | PAST |
|---|---|---|
| j'eus été etc | je serais | j'aurais été |
| | tu serais | tu aurais été |
| | il serait | il aurait été |
| | nous serions | nous aurions été |
| FUTURE PERFECT | vous seriez | vous auriez été |
| j'aurai été etc | ils seraient | ils auraient été |

## SUBJUNCTIVE

| PRESENT | IMPERFECT | PERFECT |
|---|---|---|
| je sois | je fusse | j'aie été |
| tu sois | tu fusses | tu aies été |
| il soit | il fût | il ait été |
| nous soyons | nous fussions | nous ayons été |
| vous soyez | vous fussiez | vous ayez été |
| ils soient | ils fussent | ils aient été |

| IMPERATIVE | INFINITIVE | PARTICIPLE |
|---|---|---|
| sois | PRESENT | PRESENT |
| soyons | être | étant |
| soyez | | |
| | PAST | PAST |
| | avoir été | été |

## FAIRE     to do/to make

| PRESENT | IMPERFECT | FUTURE |
|---|---|---|
| je fais | je faisais | je ferai |
| tu fais | tu faisais | tu feras |
| il fait | il faisait | il fera |
| nous faisons | nous faisions | nous ferons |
| vous faites | vous faisiez | vous ferez |
| ils font | ils faisaient | ils feront |

| PAST HISTORIC | PERFECT | PLUPERFECT |
|---|---|---|
| je fis | j'ai fait | j'avais fait |
| tu fis | tu as fait | tu avais fait |
| il fit | il a fait | il avait fait |
| nous fîmes | nous avons fait | nous avions fait |
| vous fîtes | vous avez fait | vous aviez fait |
| ils firent | ils ont fait | ils avaient fait |

## CONDITIONAL

| PAST ANTERIOR | PRESENT | PAST |
|---|---|---|
| j'eus fait etc | je ferais | j'aurais fait |
| | tu ferais | tu aurais fait |
| | il ferait | il aurait fait |
| | nous ferions | nous aurions fait |
| FUTURE PERFECT | vous feriez | vous auriez fait |
| j'aurai fait etc | ils feraient | ils auraient fait |

## SUBJUNCTIVE

| PRESENT | IMPERFECT | PERFECT |
|---|---|---|
| je fasse | je fisse | j'aie fait |
| tu fasses | tu fisses | tu aies fait |
| il fasse | il fît | il ait fait |
| nous fassions | nous fissions | nous ayons fait |
| vous fassiez | vous fissiez | vous ayez fait |
| ils fassent | ils fissent | ils aient fait |

| IMPERATIVE | INFINITIVE | PARTICIPLE |
|---|---|---|
| fais | **PRESENT** | **PRESENT** |
| faisons | faire | faisant |
| faites | | |
| | **PAST** | **PAST** |
| | avoir fait | fait |

## FALLOIR    to be necessary

| PRESENT | IMPERFECT | FUTURE |
|---|---|---|
| il faut | il fallait | il faudra |

| PAST HISTORIC | PERFECT | PLUPERFECT |
|---|---|---|
| il fallut | il a fallu | il avait fallu |

### CONDITIONAL

| PAST ANTERIOR | PRESENT | PAST |
|---|---|---|
| il eut fallu | il faudrait | il aurait fallu |

| FUTURE PERFECT | | |
|---|---|---|
| il aura fallu | | |

### SUBJUNCTIVE

| PRESENT | IMPERFECT | PERFECT |
|---|---|---|
| il faille | il fallût | il ait fallu |

| IMPERATIVE | INFINITIVE | PARTICIPLE |
|---|---|---|
| | PRESENT | PRESENT |
| | falloir | |
| | PAST | PAST |
| | avoir fallu | fallu |

# VERBS

## FINIR     to finish

| PRESENT | IMPERFECT | FUTURE |
|---|---|---|
| je finis | je finissais | je finirai |
| tu finis | tu finissais | tu finiras |
| il finit | il finissait | il finira |
| nous finissons | nous finissions | nous finirons |
| vous finissez | vous finissiez | vous finirez |
| ils finissent | ils finissaient | ils finiront |

| PAST HISTORIC | PERFECT | PLUPERFECT |
|---|---|---|
| je finis | j'ai fini | j'avais fini |
| tu finis | tu as fini | tu avais fini |
| il finit | il a fini | il avait fini |
| nous finîmes | nous avons fini | nous avions fini |
| vous finîtes | vous avez fini | vous aviez fini |
| ils finirent | ils ont fini | ils avaient fini |

## CONDITIONAL

| PAST ANTERIOR | PRESENT | PAST |
|---|---|---|
| j'eus fini etc | je finirais | j'aurais fini |
| | tu finirais | tu aurais fini |
| | il finirait | il aurait fini |
| | nous finirions | nous aurions fini |
| FUTURE PERFECT | vous finiriez | vous auriez fini |
| j'aurai fini etc | ils finiraient | ils auraient fini |

## SUBJUNCTIVE

| PRESENT | IMPERFECT | PERFECT |
|---|---|---|
| je finisse | je finisse | j'aie fini |
| tu finisses | tu finisses | tu aies fini |
| il finisse | il finît | il ait fini |
| nous finissions | nous finissions | nous ayons fini |
| vous finissiez | vous finissiez | vous ayez fini |
| ils finissent | ils finissent | ils aient fini |

| IMPERATIVE | INFINITIVE | PARTICIPLE |
|---|---|---|
| finis | **PRESENT** | **PRESENT** |
| finissons | finir | finissant |
| finissez | | |
| | **PAST** | **PAST** |
| | avoir fini | fini |

# SE MÉFIER  to be suspicious

| PRESENT | IMPERFECT | FUTURE |
|---|---|---|
| je me méfie | je me méfiais | je me méfierai |
| tu te méfies | tu te méfiais | tu te méfieras |
| il se méfie | il se méfiait | il se méfiera |
| nous nous méfions | nous nous méfiions | nous nous méfierons |
| vous vous méfiez | vous vous méfiiez | vous vous méfierez |
| ils se méfient | ils se méfiaient | ils se méfieront |

| PAST HISTORIC | PERFECT | PLUPERFECT |
|---|---|---|
| je me méfiai | je me suis méfié(e) | je m'étais méfié(e) |
| tu te méfias | tu t'es méfié(e) | tu t'étais méfié(e) |
| il se méfia | il (elle) s'est méfié(e) | il (elle) s'était méfié(e) |
| nous nous méfiâmes | nous ns. sommes méfié(e)s | nous ns. étions méfié(e)s |
| vous vous méfiâtes | vous vs. êtes méfié(e)(s) | vous vs. étiez méfié(e)(s) |
| ils se méfièrent | ils (elles) se sont méfié(e)s | ils (elles) s'étaient méfié(e)s |

## CONDITIONAL

| PAST ANTERIOR | PRESENT | PAST |
|---|---|---|
| je me fus méfié(e) etc | je me méfierais | je,me serais méfié(e) |
| | tu te méfierais | tu te serais méfié(e) |
| | il se méfierait | il (elle) se serait méfié(e) |
| | nous nous méfierions | nous ns. serions méfié(e)s |
| **FUTURE PERFECT** | vous vous méfieriez | vous vs. seriez méfié(e)(s) |
| je me serai méfié(e) etc | ils se méfieraient | ils (elles) se seraient méfié(e)s |

## SUBJUNCTIVE

| PRESENT | IMPERFECT | PERFECT |
|---|---|---|
| je me méfie | je me méfiasse | je me sois méfié(e) |
| tu te méfies | tu te méfiasses | tu te sois méfié(e) |
| il se méfie | il se méfiât | il (elle) se soit méfié(e) |
| nous nous méfiions | nous nous méfiassions | nous ns. soyons méfié(e)s |
| vous vous méfiiez | vous vous méfiassiez | vous vs. soyez méfié(e)(s) |
| ils se méfient | ils se méfiassent | ils (elles) se soient méfié(e)s |

| IMPERATIVE | INFINITIVE | PARTICIPLE |
|---|---|---|
| méfie-toi | **PRESENT** | **PRESENT** |
| méfions-nous | se méfier | se méfiant |
| méfiez-vous | | |
| | **PAST** | **PAST** |
| | s'être méfié(e)(s) | méfié |

## **METTRE** to put

| PRESENT | IMPERFECT | FUTURE |
|---|---|---|
| je mets | je mettais | je mettrai |
| tu mets | tu mettais | tu mettras |
| il met | il mettait | il mettra |
| nous mettons | nous mettions | nous mettrons |
| vous mettez | vous mettiez | vous mettrez |
| ils mettent | ils mettaient | ils mettront |

| PAST HISTORIC | PERFECT | PLUPERFECT |
|---|---|---|
| je mis | j'ai mis | j'avais mis |
| tu mis | tu as mis | tu avais mis |
| il mit | il a mis | il avait mis |
| nous mîmes | nous avons mis | nous avions mis |
| vous mîtes | vous avez mis | vous aviez mis |
| ils mirent | ils ont mis | ils avaient mis |

### CONDITIONAL

| PAST ANTERIOR | PRESENT | PAST |
|---|---|---|
| j'eus mis etc | je mettrais | j'aurais mis |
| | tu mettrais | tu aurais mis |
| | il mettrait | il aurait mis |
| | nous mettrions | nous aurions mis |
| FUTURE PERFECT | vous mettriez | vous auriez mis |
| j'aurai mis etc | ils mettraient | ils auraient mis |

### SUBJUNCTIVE

| PRESENT | IMPERFECT | PERFECT |
|---|---|---|
| je mette | je misse | j'aie mis |
| tu mettes | tu misses | tu aies mis |
| il mette | il mît | il ait mis |
| nous mettions | nous missions | nous ayons mis |
| vous mettiez | vous missiez | vous ayez mis |
| ils mettent | ils missent | ils aient mis |

| IMPERATIVE | INFINITIVE | PARTICIPLE |
|---|---|---|
| mets | PRESENT | PRESENT |
| mettons | mettre | mettant |
| mettez | | |
| | PAST | PAST |
| | avoir mis | mis |

## OUVRIR    to open

| PRESENT | IMPERFECT | FUTURE |
|---|---|---|
| j'ouvre | j'ouvrais | j'ouvrirai |
| tu ouvres | tu ouvrais | tu ouvriras |
| il ouvre | il ouvrait | il ouvrira |
| nous ouvrons | nous ouvrions | nous ouvrirons |
| vous ouvrez | vous ouvriez | vous ouvrirez |
| ils ouvrent | ils ouvraient | ils ouvriront |

| PAST HISTORIC | PERFECT | PLUPERFECT |
|---|---|---|
| j'ouvris | j'ai ouvert | j'avais ouvert |
| tu ouvris | tu as ouvert | tu avais ouvert |
| il ouvrit | il a ouvert | il avait ouvert |
| nous ouvrîmes | nous avons ouvert | nous avions ouvert |
| vous ouvrîtes | vous avez ouvert | vous aviez ouvert |
| ils ouvrirent | ils ont ouvert | ils avaient ouvert |

### CONDITIONAL

| PAST ANTERIOR | PRESENT | PAST |
|---|---|---|
| j'eus ouvert etc | j'ouvrirais | j'aurais ouvert |
| | tu ouvrirais | tu aurais ouvert |
| | il ouvrirait | il aurait ouvert |
| | nous ouvririons | nous aurions ouvert |
| FUTURE PERFECT | vous ouvririez | vous auriez ouvert |
| j'aurai ouvert etc | ils ouvriraient | ils auraient ouvert |

### SUBJUNCTIVE

| PRESENT | IMPERFECT | PERFECT |
|---|---|---|
| j'ouvre | j'ouvrisse | j'aie ouvert |
| tu ouvres | tu ouvrisses | tu aies ouvert |
| il ouvre | il ouvrît | il ait ouvert |
| nous ouvrions | nous ouvrissions | nous ayons ouvert |
| vous ouvriez | vous ouvrissiez | vous ayez ouvert |
| ils ouvrent | ils ouvrissent | ils aient ouvert |

| IMPERATIVE | INFINITIVE | PARTICIPLE |
|---|---|---|
| ouvre | PRESENT | PRESENT |
| ouvrons | ouvrir | ouvrant |
| ouvrez | | |
| | PAST | PAST |
| | avoir ouvert | ouvert |

## **POUVOIR**   to be able to

| PRESENT | IMPERFECT | FUTURE |
|---|---|---|
| je peux | je pouvais | je pourrai |
| tu peux | tu pouvais | tu pourras |
| il peut | il pouvait | il pourra |
| nous pouvons | nous pouvions | nous pourrons |
| vous pouvez | vous pouviez | vous pourrez |
| ils peuvent | ils pouvaient | ils pourront |

| PAST HISTORIC | PERFECT | PLUPERFECT |
|---|---|---|
| je pus | j'ai pu | j'avais pu |
| tu pus | tu as pu | tu avais pu |
| il put | il a pu | il avait pu |
| nous pûmes | nous avons pu | nous avions pu |
| vous pûtes | vous avez pu | vous aviez pu |
| ils purent | ils ont pu | ils avaient pu |

### CONDITIONAL

| PAST ANTERIOR | PRESENT | PAST |
|---|---|---|
| j'eus pu etc | je pourrais | j'aurais pu |
| | tu pourrais | tu aurais pu |
| | il pourrait | il aurait pu |
| | nous pourrions | nous aurions pu |
| FUTURE PERFECT | vous pourriez | vous auriez pu |
| j'aurai pu etc | ils pourraient | ils auraient pu |

### SUBJUNCTIVE

| PRESENT | IMPERFECT | PERFECT |
|---|---|---|
| je puisse | je pusse | j'aie pu |
| tu puisses | tu pusses | tu aies pu |
| il puisse | il pût | il ait pu |
| nous puissions | nous pussions | nous ayons pu |
| vous puissiez | vous pussiez | vous ayez pu |
| ils puissent | ils pussent | ils aient pu |

| IMPERATIVE | INFINITIVE | PARTICIPLE |
|---|---|---|
| | PRESENT | PRESENT |
| | pouvoir | pouvant |
| | | |
| | PAST | PAST |
| | avoir pu | pu |

# PRENDRE  to take

| PRESENT | IMPERFECT | FUTURE |
|---|---|---|
| je prends | je prenais | je prendrai |
| tu prends | tu prenais | tu prendras |
| il prend | il prenait | il prendra |
| nous prenons | nous prenions | nous prendrons |
| vous prenez | vous preniez | vous prendrez |
| ils prennent | ils prenaient | ils prendront |

| PAST HISTORIC | PERFECT | PLUPERFECT |
|---|---|---|
| je pris | j'ai pris | j'avais pris |
| tu pris | tu as pris | tu avais pris |
| il prit | il a pris | il avait pris |
| nous prîmes | nous avons pris | nous avions pris |
| vous prîtes | vous avez pris | vous aviez pris |
| ils prirent | ils ont pris | ils avaient pris |

## CONDITIONAL

| PAST ANTERIOR | PRESENT | PAST |
|---|---|---|
| j'eus pris etc | je prendrais | j'aurais pris |
| | tu prendrais | tu aurais pris |
| | il prendrait | il aurait pris |
| | nous prendrions | nous aurions pris |
| FUTURE PERFECT | vous prendriez | vous auriez pris |
| j'aurai pris etc | ils prendraient | ils auraient pris |

## SUBJUNCTIVE

| PRESENT | IMPERFECT | PERFECT |
|---|---|---|
| je prenne | je prisse | j'aie pris |
| tu prennes | tu prisses | tu aies pris |
| il prenne | il prît | il ait pris |
| nous prenions | nous prissions | nous ayons pris |
| vous preniez | vous prissiez | vous ayez pris |
| ils prennent | ils prissent | ils aient pris |

| IMPERATIVE | INFINITIVE | PARTICIPLE |
|---|---|---|
| prends | **PRESENT** | **PRESENT** |
| prenons | prendre | prenant |
| prenez | | |
| | **PAST** | **PAST** |
| | avoir pris | pris |

## **RECEVOIR**   to receive

| PRESENT | IMPERFECT | FUTURE |
|---|---|---|
| je reçois | je recevais | je recevrai |
| tu reçois | tu recevais | tu recevras |
| il reçoit | il recevait | il recevra |
| nous recevons | nous recevions | nous recevrons |
| vous recevez | vous receviez | vous recevrez |
| ils reçoivent | ils recevaient | ils recevront |

| PAST HISTORIC | PERFECT | PLUPERFECT |
|---|---|---|
| je reçus | j'ai reçu | j'avais reçu |
| tu reçus | tu as reçu | tu avais reçu |
| il reçut | il a reçu | il avait reçu |
| nous reçûmes | nous avons reçu | nous avions reçu |
| vous reçûtes | vous avez reçu | vous aviez reçu |
| ils reçurent | ils ont reçu | ils avaient reçu |

### CONDITIONAL

| PAST ANTERIOR | PRESENT | PAST |
|---|---|---|
| j'eus reçu etc | je recevrais | j'aurais reçu |
| | tu recevrais | tu aurais reçu |
| | il recevrait | il aurait reçu |
| | nous recevrions | nous aurions reçu |
| FUTURE PERFECT | vous recevriez | vous auriez reçu |
| j'aurai reçu etc | ils recevraient | ils auraient reçu |

### SUBJUNCTIVE

| PRESENT | IMPERFECT | PERFECT |
|---|---|---|
| je reçoive | je reçusse | j'aie reçu |
| tu reçoives | tu reçusses | tu aies reçu |
| il reçoive | il reçût | il ait reçu |
| nous recevions | nous reçussions | nous ayons reçu |
| vous receviez | vous reçussiez | vous ayez reçu |
| ils reçoivent | ils reçussent | ils aient reçu |

| IMPERATIVE | INFINITIVE | PARTICIPLE |
|---|---|---|
| reçois | PRESENT | PRESENT |
| recevons | recevoir | recevant |
| recevez | | |
| | PAST | PAST |
| | avoir reçu | reçu |

# SAVOIR  to know

| PRESENT | IMPERFECT | FUTURE |
|---|---|---|
| je sais | je savais | je saurai |
| tu sais | tu savais | tu sauras |
| il sait | il savait | il saura |
| nous savons | nous savions | nous saurons |
| vous savez | vous saviez | vous saurez |
| ils savent | ils savaient | ils sauront |

| PAST HISTORIC | PERFECT | PLUPERFECT |
|---|---|---|
| je sus | j'ai su | j'avais su |
| tu sus | tu as su | tu avais su |
| il sut | il a su | il avait su |
| nous sûmes | nous avons su | nous avions su |
| vous sûtes | vous avez su | vous aviez su |
| ils surent | ils ont su | ils avaient su |

## CONDITIONAL

| PAST ANTERIOR | PRESENT | PAST |
|---|---|---|
| j'eus su etc | je saurais | j'aurais su |
| | tu saurais | tu aurais su |
| | il saurait | il aurait su |
| | nous saurions | nous aurions su |
| FUTURE PERFECT | vous sauriez | vous auriez su |
| j'aurai su etc | ils sauraient | ils auraient su |

## SUBJUNCTIVE

| PRESENT | IMPERFECT | PERFECT |
|---|---|---|
| je sache | je susse | j'aie su |
| tu saches | tu susses | tu aies su |
| il sache | il sût | il ait su |
| nous sachions | nous sussions | nous ayons su |
| vous sachiez | vous sussiez | vous ayez su |
| ils sachent | ils sussent | ils aient su |

| IMPERATIVE | INFINITIVE | PARTICIPLE |
|---|---|---|
| sache | PRESENT | PRESENT |
| sachons | savoir | sachant |
| sachez | | |
| | PAST | PAST |
| | avoir su | su |

## TENIR   to hold

| PRESENT | IMPERFECT | FUTURE |
|---|---|---|
| je tiens | je tenais | je tiendrai |
| tu tiens | tu tenais | tu tiendras |
| il tient | il tenait | il tiendra |
| nous tenons | nous tenions | nous tiendrons |
| vous tenez | vous teniez | vous tiendrez |
| ils tiennent | ils tenaient | ils tiendront |

| PAST HISTORIC | PERFECT | PLUPERFECT |
|---|---|---|
| je tins | j'ai tenu | j'avais tenu |
| tu tins | tu as tenu | tu avais tenu |
| il tint | il a tenu | il avait tenu |
| nous tînmes | nous avons tenu | nous avions tenu |
| vous tîntes | vous avez tenu | vous aviez tenu |
| ils tinrent | ils ont tenu | ils avaient tenu |

### CONDITIONAL

| PAST ANTERIOR | PRESENT | PAST |
|---|---|---|
| j'eus tenu etc | je tiendrais | j'aurais tenu |
| | tu tiendrais | tu aurais tenu |
| | il tiendrait | il aurait tenu |
| | nous tiendrions | nous aurions tenu |
| FUTURE PERFECT | vous tiendriez | vous auriez tenu |
| j'aurai tenu etc | ils tiendraient | ils auraient tenu |

### SUBJUNCTIVE

| PRESENT | IMPERFECT | PERFECT |
|---|---|---|
| je tienne | je tinsse | j'aie tenu |
| tu tiennes | tu tinsses | tu aies tenu |
| il tienne | il tînt | il ait tenu |
| nous tenions | nous tinssions | nous ayons tenu |
| vous teniez | vous tinssiez | vous ayez tenu |
| ils tiennent | ils tinssent | ils aient tenu |

| IMPERATIVE | INFINITIVE | PARTICIPLE |
|---|---|---|
| tiens | PRESENT | PRESENT |
| tenons | tenir | tenant |
| tenez | | |
| | PAST | PAST |
| | avoir tenu | tenu |

# **VENDRE**   to sell

| PRESENT | IMPERFECT | FUTURE |
|---|---|---|
| je vends | je vendais | je vendrai |
| tu vends | tu vendais | tu vendras |
| il vend | il vendait | il vendra |
| nous vendons | nous vendions | nous vendrons |
| vous vendez | vous vendiez | vous vendrez |
| ils vendent | ils vendaient | ils vendront |

| PAST HISTORIC | PERFECT | PLUPERFECT |
|---|---|---|
| je vendis | j'ai vendu | j'avais vendu |
| tu vendis | tu as vendu | tu avais vendu |
| il vendit | il a vendu | il avait vendu |
| nous vendîmes | nous avons vendu | nous avions vendu |
| vous vendîtes | vous avez vendu | vous aviez vendu |
| ils vendirent | ils ont vendu | ils avaient vendu |

## CONDITIONAL

| PAST ANTERIOR | PRESENT | PAST |
|---|---|---|
| j'eus vendu etc | je vendrais | j'aurais vendu |
| | tu vendrais | tu aurais vendu |
| | il vendrait | il aurait vendu |
| | nous vendrions | nous aurions vendu |
| FUTURE PERFECT | vous vendriez | vous auriez vendu |
| j'aurai vendu etc | ils vendraient | ils auraient vendu |

## SUBJUNCTIVE

| PRESENT | IMPERFECT | PERFECT |
|---|---|---|
| je vende | je vendisse | j'aie vendu |
| tu vendes | tu vendisses | tu aies vendu |
| il vende | il vendît | il ait vendu |
| nous vendions | nous vendissions | nous ayons vendu |
| vous vendiez | vous vendissiez | vous ayez vendu |
| ils vendent | ils vendissent | ils aient vendu |

| IMPERATIVE | INFINITIVE | PARTICIPLE |
|---|---|---|
| vends | PRESENT | PRESENT |
| vendons | vendre | vendant |
| vendez | | |
| | PAST | PAST |
| | avoir vendu | vendu |

# VERBS

## VENIR — to come

| PRESENT | IMPERFECT | FUTURE |
|---|---|---|
| je viens | je venais | je viendrai |
| tu viens | tu venais | tu viendras |
| il vient | il venait | il viendra |
| nous venons | nous venions | nous viendrons |
| vous venez | vous veniez | vous viendrez |
| ils viennent | ils venaient | ils viendront |

| PAST HISTORIC | PERFECT | PLUPERFECT |
|---|---|---|
| je vins | je suis venu(e) | j'étais venu(e) |
| tu vins | tu es venu(e) | tu étais venu(e) |
| il vint | il (elle) est venu(e) | il (elle) était venu(e) |
| nous vînmes | nous sommes venu(e)s | nous étions venu(e)s |
| vous vîntes | vous êtes venu(e)(s) | vous étiez venu(e)(s) |
| ils vinrent | ils (elles) sont venu(e)s | ils (elles) étaient venu(e)s |

### CONDITIONAL

| | PRESENT | PAST |
|---|---|---|
| PAST ANTERIOR | je viendrais | je serais venu(e) |
| je fus venu(e) etc | tu viendrais | tu serais venu(e) |
| | il viendrait | il (elle) serait venu(e) |
| | nous viendrions | nous serions venu(e)s |
| FUTURE PERFECT | vous viendriez | vous seriez venu(e)(s) |
| je serai venu(e) etc | ils viendraient | ils (elles) seraient venu(e)s |

### SUBJUNCTIVE

| PRESENT | IMPERFECT | PERFECT |
|---|---|---|
| je vienne | je vinsse | je sois venu(e) |
| tu viennes | tu vinsses | tu sois venu(e) |
| il vienne | il vînt | il (elle) soit venu(e) |
| nous venions | nous vinssions | nous soyons venu(e)s |
| vous veniez | vous vinssiez | vous soyez venu(e)(s) |
| ils viennent | ils vinssent | ils (elles) soient venu(e)s |

| IMPERATIVE | INFINITIVE | PARTICIPLE |
|---|---|---|
| viens | PRESENT | PRESENT |
| venons | venir | venant |
| venez | | |
| | PAST | PAST |
| | être venu(e)(s) | venu |

# **VIVRE**   to live

| PRESENT | IMPERFECT | FUTURE |
|---|---|---|
| je vis | je vivais | je vivrai |
| tu vis | tu vivais | tu vivras |
| il vit | il vivait | il vivra |
| nous vivons | nous vivions | nous vivrons |
| vous vivez | vous viviez | vous vivrez |
| ils vivent | ils vivaient | ils vivront |

| PAST HISTORIC | PERFECT | PLUPERFECT |
|---|---|---|
| je vécus | j'ai vécu | j'avais vécu |
| tu vécus | tu as vécu | tu avais vécu |
| il vécut | il a vécu | il avait vécu |
| nous vécûmes | nous avons vécu | nous avions vécu |
| vous vécûtes | vous avez vécu | vous aviez vécu |
| ils vécurent | ils ont vécu | ils avaient vécu |

## CONDITIONAL

| PAST ANTERIOR | PRESENT | PAST |
|---|---|---|
| j'eus vécu etc | je vivrais | j'aurais vécu |
| | tu vivrais | tu aurais vécu |
| | il vivrait | il aurait vécu |
| | nous vivrions | nous aurions vécu |
| **FUTURE PERFECT** | vous vivriez | vous auriez vécu |
| j'aurai vécu etc | ils vivraient | ils auraient vécu |

## SUBJUNCTIVE

| PRESENT | IMPERFECT | PERFECT |
|---|---|---|
| je vive | je vécusse | j'aie vécu |
| tu vives | tu vécusses | tu aies vécu |
| il vive | il vécût | il ait vécu |
| nous vivions | nous vécussions | nous ayons vécu |
| vous viviez | vous vécussiez | vous ayez vécu |
| ils vivent | ils vécussent | ils aient vécu |

| IMPERATIVE | INFINITIVE | PARTICIPLE |
|---|---|---|
| vis | **PRESENT** | **PRESENT** |
| vivons | vivre | vivant |
| vivez | | |
| | **PAST** | **PAST** |
| | avoir vécu | vécu |

# VOIR    to see

| PRESENT | IMPERFECT | FUTURE |
|---|---|---|
| je vois | je voyais | je verrai |
| tu vois | tu voyais | tu verras |
| il voit | il voyait | il verra |
| nous voyons | nous voyions | nous verrons |
| vous voyez | vous voyiez | vous verrez |
| ils voient | ils voyaient | ils verront |

| PAST HISTORIC | PERFECT | PLUPERFECT |
|---|---|---|
| je vis | j'ai vu | j'avais vu |
| tu vis | tu as vu | tu avais vu |
| il vit | il a vu | il avait vu |
| nous vîmes | nous avons vu | nous avions vu |
| vous vîtes | vous avez vu | vous aviez vu |
| ils virent | ils ont vu | ils avaient vu |

## CONDITIONAL

| PAST ANTERIOR | PRESENT | PAST |
|---|---|---|
| j'eus vu etc | je verrais | j'aurais vu |
| | tu verrais | tu aurais vu |
| | il verrait | il aurait vu |
| | nous verrions | nous aurions vu |
| FUTURE PERFECT | vous verriez | vous auriez vu |
| j'aurai vu etc | ils verraient | ils auraient vu |

## SUBJUNCTIVE

| PRESENT | IMPERFECT | PERFECT |
|---|---|---|
| je voie | je visse | j'aie vu |
| tu voies | tu visses | tu aies vu |
| il voie | il vît | il ait vu |
| nous voyions | nous vissions | nous ayons vu |
| vous voyiez | vous vissiez | vous ayez vu |
| ils voient | ils vissent | ils aient vu |

| IMPERATIVE | INFINITIVE | PARTICIPLE |
|---|---|---|
| vois | PRESENT | PRESENT |
| voyons | voir | voyant |
| voyez | | |
| | PAST | PAST |
| | avoir vu | vu |

## **VOULOIR** to want

| PRESENT | IMPERFECT | FUTURE |
|---|---|---|
| je veux | je voulais | je voudrai |
| tu veux | tu voulais | tu voudras |
| il veut | il voulait | il voudra |
| nous voulons | nous voulions | nous voudrons |
| vous voulez | vous vouliez | vous voudrez |
| ils veulent | ils voulaient | ils voudront |

| PAST HISTORIC | PERFECT | PLUPERFECT |
|---|---|---|
| je voulus | j'ai voulu | j'avais voulu |
| tu voulus | tu as voulu | tu avais voulu |
| il voulut | il a voulu | il avait voulu |
| nous voulûmes | nous avons voulu | nous avions voulu |
| vous voulûtes | vous avez voulu | vous aviez voulu |
| ils voulurent | ils ont voulu | ils avaient voulu |

### CONDITIONAL

| PAST ANTERIOR | PRESENT | PAST |
|---|---|---|
| j'eus voulu etc | je voudrais | j'aurais voulu |
|  | tu voudrais | tu aurais voulu |
|  | il voudrait | il aurait voulu |
|  | nous voudrions | nous aurions voulu |
| FUTURE PERFECT | vous voudriez | vous auriez voulu |
| j'aurai voulu etc | ils voudraient | ils auraient voulu |

### SUBJUNCTIVE

| PRESENT | IMPERFECT | PERFECT |
|---|---|---|
| je veuille | je voulusse | j'aie voulu |
| tu veuilles | tu voulusses | tu aies voulu |
| il veuille | il voulût | il ait voulu |
| nous voulions | nous voulussions | nous ayons voulu |
| vous vouliez | vous voulussiez | vous ayez voulu |
| ils veuillent | ils voulussent | ils aient voulu |

| IMPERATIVE | INFINITIVE | PARTICIPLE |
|---|---|---|
| veuille | **PRESENT** | **PRESENT** |
| veuillons | vouloir | voulant |
| veuillez |  |  |
|  | **PAST** | **PAST** |
|  | avoir voulu | voulu |

## M. Verbal Constructions

There are two main types of verbal construction:

### 1. Verbs followed by an infinitive

There are three main types of construction when a verb is followed by an infinitive. For examples of all three types, see pp 146-54.

**a)** *Verbs followed by an infinitive without any linking preposition*

These include verbs of wishing and willing, of movement and of perception:

| | | |
|---|---|---|
| **adorer**<br>to love | **aimer**<br>to like | **aimer mieux**<br>to prefer |
| **aller**<br>to go (and) | **compter**<br>to intend to | **descendre**<br>to go down (and) |
| **désirer**<br>to wish | **détester**<br>to hate | **devoir**<br>to have to |
| **écouter**<br>to listen to | **entendre**<br>to hear | **entrer**<br>to go in (and) |
| **envoyer**<br>to send | **espérer**<br>to hope to | **faire**<br>to make |
| **falloir**<br>to have to | **laisser**<br>to let | **monter**<br>to go up (and) |
| **oser**<br>to dare | **pouvoir**<br>to be able to | **préférer**<br>to prefer to |
| **regarder**<br>to watch | **rentrer**<br>to go in/back (and) | **savoir**<br>to know how to |
| **sembler**<br>to seem to | **sentir**<br>to feel | **sortir**<br>to go out (and) |
| **souhaiter**<br>to wish to | **valoir mieux**<br>to be better to | **venir**<br>to come (and) |
| **voir**<br>to see | **vouloir**<br>to want to | |

**b)** *Verbs followed by à + infinitive*

| | |
|---|---|
| aider à | to help (to do) |
| s'amuser à | to enjoy (doing) |
| apprendre à | to learn (to do) |
| s'apprêter à | to get ready (to do) |
| arriver à | to manage (to do) |
| s'attendre à | to expect (to do) |
| autoriser à | to allow (to do) |
| chercher à | to try (to do) |
| commencer à | to start (doing) |
| consentir à | to agree (to do) |
| consister à | to consist in (doing) |
| continuer à | to continue (to do) |
| se décider à | to make up one's mind (to do) |
| encourager à | to encourage (to do) |
| enseigner à | to teach how (to do) |
| forcer à | to force (to do) |
| s'habituer à | to get used (to doing) |
| hésiter à | to hesitate (to do) |
| inciter à | to prompt (to do) |
| s'intéresser à | to be interested in (doing) |
| inviter à | to invite (to do) |
| se mettre à | to start (doing) |
| obliger à | to force (to do) |
| parvenir à | to succeed (in doing) |
| passer son temps à | to spend one's time (doing) |
| perdre son temps à | to waste one's time (doing) |
| persister à | to persist in (doing) |
| pousser à | to urge (to do) |
| se préparer à | to get ready (to do) |
| renoncer à | to give up (doing) |
| rester à | to be left (to do) |
| réussir à | to manage (to do) |
| servir à | to be used for (doing) |
| songer à | to think of (doing) |
| tarder à | to delay/be late in (doing) |
| tenir à | to be keen (to do) |

c) *Verbs followed by de + infinitive:*

| | |
|---|---|
| accepter de | to agree (to do) |
| accuser de | to accuse of (doing) |
| achever de | to finish (doing) |
| s'arrêter de | to stop (doing) |
| avoir besoin de | to need (to do) |
| avoir envie de | to feel like (doing) |
| avoir peur de | to be afraid (to do) |
| cesser de | to stop (doing) |
| se charger de | to undertake (to do) |
| commander de | to order (to do) |
| conseiller de | to advise (to do) |
| se contenter de | to make do with (doing) |
| craindre de | to be afraid (to do) |
| décider de | to decide (to do) |
| déconseiller de | to advise against (doing) |
| défendre de | to forbid (to do) |
| demander de | to ask (to do) |
| se dépêcher de | to hasten (to do) |
| dire de | to tell (to do) |
| dissuader de | to dissuade from (doing) |
| s'efforcer de | to strive (to do) |
| empêcher de | to prevent (from doing) |
| s'empresser de | to hasten (to do) |
| entreprendre de | to undertake (to do) |
| essayer de | to try (to do) |
| s'étonner de | to be surprised (at doing) |
| éviter de | to avoid (doing) |
| s'excuser de | to apologize for (doing) |
| faire semblant de | to pretend (to do) |
| feindre de | to pretend (to do) |
| finir de | to finish (doing) |
| se garder de | to be careful not to (do) |
| se hâter de | to hasten (to do) |
| interdire de | to forbid (to do) |
| jurer de | to swear (to do) |
| manquer de | 'to nearly' (do) |
| menacer de | to threaten (to do) |
| mériter de | to deserve (to do) |
| négliger de | to fail (to do) |

| | |
|---|---|
| s'occuper de | to undertake (to do) |
| offrir de | to offer (to do) |
| omettre de | to omit (to do) |
| ordonner de | to order (to do) |
| oublier de | to forget (to do) |
| permettre de | to allow (to do) |
| persuader de | to persuade (to do) |
| prier de | to ask (to do) |
| promettre de | to promise (to do) |
| proposer de | to offer (to do) |
| recommander de | to recommend (to do) |
| refuser de | to refuse (to do) |
| regretter de | to be sorry (to do) |
| remercier de | to thank for (doing) |
| résoudre de | to resolve (to do) |
| risquer de | to risk (doing) |
| se souvenir de | to remember (doing) |
| suggérer de | to suggest (doing) |
| supplier de | to implore (to do) |
| tâcher de | to try (to do) |
| tenter de | to try (to do) |
| venir de | to have just (done) |

## 2. Verbs followed by an object

In general, verbs which take a direct object in French also take a direct object in English, and verbs which take an indirect object in French (ie verb + preposition + object) also take an indirect object in English.

There are, however, some exceptions:

a) *Verbs followed by an indirect object in English but not in French* (the English preposition is not translated):

| | |
|---|---|
| attendre | to wait for |
| chercher | to look for |
| demander | to ask for |
| écouter | to listen to |
| espérer | to hope for |
| payer | to pay for |
| regarder | to look at |
| reprocher | to blame for |

on a demandé l'addition
we asked for the bill

je cherche mon frère
I'm looking for my brother

j'attendais l'autobus
I was waiting for the bus

tu écoutes la radio?
are you listening to the radio?

**b)** *Verbs which take a direct object in English, but an indirect object in French:*

| | |
|---|---|
| convenir à | to suit |
| se fier à | to trust |
| jouer à | to play *(game, sport)* |
| jouer de | to play *(musical instrument)* |
| obéir à | to obey |
| désobéir à | to disobey |
| pardonner à | to forgive |
| renoncer à | to give up |
| répondre à | to answer |
| résister à | to resist |
| ressembler à | to resemble (to look like) |
| téléphoner à | to phone |

tu peux te fier à moi
you can trust me

il joue bien de la guitare
he plays the guitar well

téléphonons au médecin
let's phone the doctor

tu joues souvent au tennis?
do you often play tennis?

tu as répondu à ma lettre?
did you answer my letter?

obéis à ton père!
obey your father!

**c)** *Verbs which take a direct object in English but **de** + indirect object in French:*

| | |
|---|---|
| s'apercevoir de | to notice |
| s'approcher de | to come near |
| avoir besoin de | to need |
| changer de | to change |
| douter de | to doubt |
| se douter de | to suspect |
| s'emparer de | to seize, to grab |
| jouir de | to enjoy |
| manquer de | to lack, to miss |
| se méfier de | to mistrust |
| se servir de | to use |
| se souvenir de | to remember |
| se tromper de ... | to get the wrong ... |

**je dois changer de train?**
do I have to change trains?

**il ne s'est aperçu de rien**
he didn't notice anything

**méfiez-vous de lui**
don't trust him

**je me servirai de ton vélo**
I'll use your bike

**tu te souviens de Jean?**
do you remember Jean?

**il s'est trompé de numéro**
he got the wrong number

d) *Some verbs take à or de before an object, whereas their English equivalent uses a different preposition:*

i) Verb + **à** + object:

| | |
|---|---|
| **croire à** | to believe in |
| **s'intéresser à** | to be interested in |
| **penser à** | to think of/about |
| **songer à** | to think of |
| **rêver à** | to dream of/about |
| **servir à** | to be used for |

**je m'intéresse au football et à la course automobile**
I'm interested in football and in motor-racing

**à quoi penses-tu?**
what are you thinking about?

**ça sert à quoi?**
what is this used for?

ii) Verb + **de** + object:

| | |
|---|---|
| **dépendre de** | to depend on |
| **être fâché de** | to be annoyed at |
| **féliciter de** | to congratulate for |
| **parler de** | to speak of/about |
| **remercier de** | to thank for |
| **rire de** | to laugh at |
| **traiter de** | to deal with, to be about |
| **vivre de** | to live on |

**cela dépendra du temps**
it'll depend on the weather

**il m'a parlé de toi**
he told me about you

**tu l'as remercié du cadeau qu'il t'a fait?**
did you thank him for the present he gave you?

### 3. Verbs followed by one direct object and one indirect object

a) In general, these are verbs of giving or lending, and their English equivalents are constructed in the same way, eg:

> **donner quelque chose à quelqu'un**
> to give something to someone

> **il a vendu son ordinateur à son voisin**
> he sold his computer to his neighbour

Note that after such verbs, the preposition 'to' is often omitted in English but **à**, however, cannot be omitted in French. Particular care must be taken when object pronouns are used with these verbs (see pp 80-1).

b) With verbs expressing 'taking away', **à** is translated by 'from' (**qn** stands for 'quelqu'un' and **sb** for 'somebody'):

| | |
|---|---|
| acheter à qn | to buy from sb |
| cacher à qn | to hide from sb |
| demander à qn | to ask sb for |
| emprunter à qn | to borrow from sb |
| enlever à qn | to take away from sb |
| ôter à qn | to take away from sb |
| prendre à qn | to take from sb |
| voler à qn | to steal from sb |

> **à qui as-tu emprunté cela?**    **il l'a volé à son frère**
> who did you borrow this from?    he stole it from his brother

### 4. Verb + indirect object + 'de' + infinitive

Some verbs which take a direct object in English are followed by **à** + object + **de** + infinitive in French:

| | |
|---|---|
| commander à qn de faire | to order sb to do |
| conseiller à qn de faire | to advise sb to do |
| défendre à qn de faire | to forbid sb to do |
| demander à qn de faire | to ask sb to do |
| dire à qn de faire | to tell sb to do |
| ordonner à qn de faire | to order sb to do |
| permettre à qn de faire | to allow sb to do |
| promettre à qn de faire | to promise sb to do |
| proposer à qn de faire | to offer to do for sb, to suggest to sb to do |

**je leur ai conseillé de ne pas essayer**
I advised them not to try

**demande à ton fils de t'aider**
ask your son to help you

**j'ai promis à mes parents de ne jamais recommencer**
I promised my parents never to do this again

# 8. PREPOSITIONS

Prepositions in both French and English can have many different meanings, which presents considerable difficulties for the translator. The following guide to the most common prepositions sets out the generally accepted meanings on the left, with a description of their use in brackets, and an illustration. The main meanings are given first. Prepositions are listed in alphabetical order.

## • à •

| | | |
|---|---|---|
| *at* | (place) | **au troisième arrêt**<br>at the third stop |
| | (date) | **à Noël**<br>at Christmas |
| | (time) | **à trois heures**<br>at three o'clock |
| | (idiom) | **au hasard**<br>at random<br>**au travail**<br>at work |
| *in* | (place) | **à Montmartre**<br>in Montmartre<br>**à Lyon**<br>in Lyons<br>**au supermarché**<br>in the supermarket<br>**à la campagne**<br>in the country<br>**au lit**<br>in bed<br>**au loin**<br>in the distance |
| | (manner) | **à la française**<br>in the French way |

|  |  | **à ma façon**<br>my way |
|---|---|---|
| *to* | (place) | **aller au théâtre**<br>to go to the theatre<br>**aller à Londres**<br>to go to London |
|  | (+ infinitive) | **c'est facile à faire**<br>it is easy to do *(see pp 150-1)* |
| *away from* | (distance) | **à 3 km d'ici**<br>3 km away |
| *by* | (means) | **aller à vélo**<br>to go by bike<br>**je l'ai reconnu à ses habits**<br>I recognized him by his clothing |
|  | (manner) | **fait à la main**<br>hand-made |
|  | (rate) | **à la centaine**<br>by the hundred<br>**100 km à l'heure**<br>100 km per hour |
| *for/up to* | (+ pronoun) | **c'est à vous de jouer**<br>it's your turn<br>**c'est à nous de te le dire**<br>it's up to us to tell you |
|  | (purpose) | **une tasse à café**<br>a coffee cup |
| *from* |  | **il l'a caché à ses parents**<br>he hid it from his parents |
| *his/her/my etc* | (possessive) | **son sac à elle**<br>her bag |
| *on* | (means) | **aller à cheval/à pied**<br>to go on horseback/on foot |

# PREPOSITIONS

|   | (place) | **à la page 12**<br>on page 12<br>**à droite/à gauche**<br>on/to the right/left |
|---|---|---|
|   | (time) | **à cette occasion**<br>on this occasion |
| with | (descriptive) | **un homme aux cheveux blonds**<br>a man with blond hair<br>**l'homme à la valise**<br>the man with the case |
|   | (idiom) | **à bras ouverts**<br>with open arms |

*For use of the preposition **à** with the infinitive see verbal constructions p 201.*

---

## • après •

| after | (time) | **après votre arrivée**<br>after your arrival |
|---|---|---|
|   | (sequence) | **24 ans après la mort du président**<br>24 years after the death of the President<br>**je suis allé au lit après avoir fini le livre**<br>I went to bed after I finished the book<br>**après s'être séparée de son mari**<br>after separating from her husband |

## • auprès de •

| beside | **il s'assit auprès de sa mère**<br>he sat down beside his mother |
|---|---|
| compared to | **ce n'est rien auprès de ce que tu as fait**<br>it's nothing compared to what you've done |

## .avant.

| | | |
|---|---|---|
| *before* | (time) | **avant cet après-midi**<br>before this afternoon<br>**avant ce soir**<br>before tonight<br>**avant de s'asseoir**<br>before sitting down |
| | (preference) | **la famille avant tout**<br>the family comes first (above all else) |

## .avec.

| | | |
|---|---|---|
| *with* | (association) | **je viendrai avec lui**<br>I'll come with him |
| | (means) | **elle marche avec une canne**<br>she walks with a stick |

## .chez.

| | | |
|---|---|---|
| *at* | (place) | **chez moi/toi**<br>at/to my/your house<br>**chez mon oncle**<br>at my uncle's<br>**chez le pharmacien**<br>at the chemist's |
| *among* | | **chez les Écossais**<br>among the Scots |
| *about* | | **ce qui m'énerve chez toi, c'est …**<br>what annoys me about you is … |
| *in* | | **chez Sartre**<br>in Sartre's work |

## .contre.

| | | |
|---|---|---|
| *against* | (place) | **contre le mur**<br>against the wall |

# PREPOSITIONS

| | | |
|---|---|---|
| *with* | (after verb) | **je suis fâché contre elle**<br>I'm angry with her |
| *for* | | **elle a échangé un billet contre des pièces**<br>she changed a note for coins |

## .dans.

| | | |
|---|---|---|
| *in* | (position) | **dans ma serviette**<br>in my briefcase |
| | (time) | **je pars dans deux jours**<br>I'm leaving in two days' time |
| | (idiom) | **dans l'attente de vous voir**<br>looking forward to seeing you |
| *from* | (removal) | **prendre quelque chose dans l'armoire**<br>to take something from the cupboard |
| *on* | (position) | **dans le train**<br>on the train |
| *out of* | (idiom) | **boire dans un verre**<br>to drink out of a glass |

## .de.

| | | |
|---|---|---|
| *from* | (place) | **je suis venu de Glasgow**<br>I have come from Glasgow |
| | (date) | **du 5 février au 10 mars**<br>from 5 February to 10 March<br>**d'un week-end à l'autre**<br>from one weekend to another |
| *of* | (adjectival) | **un cri de triomphe**<br>a shout of triumph |
| | (contents) | **une tasse de café**<br>a cup of coffee |

| | | | |
|---|---|---|---|
| | (cause) | **mourir de faim** | to die of hunger |
| | (measurement) | **long de 3 mètres** | 3 metres long |
| | (time) | **ma montre retarde de 10 minutes** | my watch is 10 minutes slow |
| | (price) | **le montant est de 20 euros** | the total is 20 euros |
| | (possessive) | **la père de mon ami** | my friend's father |
| | (adjectival) | **les vacances de Pâques** | the Easter holidays |
| | (after 'quelque chose') | **quelque chose de bon** | something good |
| | (after 'rien') | **rien de nouveau** | nothing new |
| | (after 'personne') | **personne d'autre** | nobody else |
| | (quantity) | **beaucoup de, peu de** | many, few |
| *by* | (idiom) | **je le connais de vue** | I know him by sight |
| *in* | (manner) | **de cette façon** | in this way |
| | (after superlatives) | **la plus haute montagne d'Écosse** | the highest mountain in Scotland |
| *on* | (position) | **de ce côté** | on this side |
| *than* | (comparative) | **moins de 2 euros** | less than 2 euros |
| | | **plus de 3 litres** | more than 3 litres |

# PREPOSITIONS

| | | |
|---|---|---|
| *to* | (after adjectives) | **ravi de vous voir**<br>delighted to see you<br>**il est facile de se tromper**<br>it is easy to make a mistake |
| | (after verbs) | **s'efforcer de**<br>to try to |
| *with* | (cause) | **tomber de fatigue**<br>to drop with exhaustion |

## .depuis.

| | | |
|---|---|---|
| *for* | (time) | **j'étudie le français depuis 3 ans**<br>I have been studying French for 3 years<br>**j'étudiais le français depuis 3 ans**<br>I had been studying French for 3 years<br>**je n'y ai pas joué depuis des années**<br>I haven't played for years |
| *from* | (place) | **depuis ma fenêtre, je vois la mer**<br>from my window I can see the sea |
| | (time) | **depuis le matin jusqu'au soir**<br>from morning till evening |
| *since* | | **depuis dimanche**<br>since Sunday |

## .derrière.

| | | |
|---|---|---|
| *behind* | (place) | **derrière la maison**<br>behind the house |

## .dès.

| | | |
|---|---|---|
| *from* | (time) | **dès six heures**<br>from six o'clock onwards<br>**dès 1934**<br>as far back as 1934<br>**dès le début**<br>from the beginning |

| | | **dès maintenant**<br>from now on |
|---|---|---|
| | (place) | **dès Édimbourg**<br>from (the moment of leaving) Edinburgh |

## .devant.

| | | |
|---|---|---|
| *in front of* | (place) | **devant l'école**<br>in front of the school |
| *before* | (place) | **sur la table devant eux**<br>on the table before them |

## .en.

| | | |
|---|---|---|
| *in* | (place) | **être en ville**<br>to be in town<br>**en Angleterre**<br>in England |
| | (colour) | **un mur peint en jaune**<br>a wall painted yellow |
| | (material) | **une montre en or**<br>a gold watch |
| *by* | (means) | **en auto/en avion**<br>by car/by plane |
| | (dates, seasons) | **en quelle année?**<br>in what year?<br>**en 2002**<br>in 2002<br>**en été**<br>in the summer<br>**en juillet**<br>in July |
| | (dress) | **en jupe**<br>in a skirt |
| | (language) | **en chinois**<br>in Chinese |

| | | |
|---|---|---|
| | (time) | **j'ai fait mes devoirs en 20 minutes**<br>I did my homework in 20 minutes |
| *like, as* | | **il s'est habillé en femme**<br>he dressed as a woman |
| *on* | (idiom) | **en vacances**<br>on holiday<br>**en moyenne**<br>on average |
| | (+ present<br>participle) | **en faisant**<br>on/while/by doing |

*Note that **en** is not used with the definite article except in certain expressions:*
**en l'an 2020** *(in the year 2020),* **en l'honneur de** *(in honour of) and* **en la présence de** *(in the presence of).*

## .en tant que.

| | |
|---|---|
| *as/in one's capacity as* | **en tant que professeur**<br>as a teacher |

## .entre.

| | | |
|---|---|---|
| *among* | | **être entre amis**<br>to be among friends |
| *between* | (place) | **entre Londres et Paris**<br>between London and Paris |
| | (time) | **entre 6 et 10 heures**<br>between 6 and 10 o'clock |
| | (idiom) | **entre nous**<br>between you and me |
| *in* | (punctuation) | **entre guillemets**<br>in inverted commas<br>**entre parenthèses**<br>in brackets |

## .d'entre.

| | |
|---|---|
| *of/from among* | **certains d'entre eux**<br>some of them |

## .envers.

| | |
|---|---|
| *to/towards* | **être bien disposé envers quelqu'un**<br>to be well-disposed towards someone |

## .hors de.

| | |
|---|---|
| *out of* | **hors de danger**<br>out of danger |

## .jusque.

| | | |
|---|---|---|
| *up to/as far as* | (place) | **jusqu'à la frontière espagnole**<br>as far as the Spanish border |
| | (time) | **jusqu'ici**<br>up to now<br>**jusque-là**<br>up till then |
| *till* | | **jusqu'à demain**<br>till tomorrow |

## .malgré.

| | |
|---|---|
| *in spite of* | **malgré la chaleur**<br>in spite of the heat |

## .par.

| | | |
|---|---|---|
| *by* | (agent) | **la décision fut prise par le président**<br>the decision was made by the President |
| | (means of<br>transport) | **par le train**<br>by train |
| | (distributive) | **trois fois par semaine**<br>three times a week<br>**deux par deux**<br>two by two |
| | (place) | **par ici/là**<br>this/that way |

| *in/on* | (weather) | **par un temps pareil**<br>in such weather<br>**par un beau jour d'hiver**<br>on a beautiful winter's day |
| *through/out of* | (place) | **regarder par la fenêtre**<br>to look out of the window<br>**jette-le par la fenêtre**<br>throw it out of the window |
| *to/on* | | **tomber par terre**<br>to fall to the ground<br>**étendu par terre**<br>lying on the ground |
| | (+ infinitive) | **commencer/finir par faire**<br>to begin/end by doing |

## .parmi.

| *among* | **parmi mes ennemis**<br>among my enemies |

## .pendant.

| *for* | (time) | **il l'avait fait pendant 5 ans**<br>he had done it for 5 years |
| *during* | | **pendant l'été**<br>during the summer |

## .pour.

| *for* | | **ce livre est pour vous**<br>this book is for you<br>**mourir pour la patrie**<br>to die for one's country |
| | (purpose) | **c'est pour cela que je suis venu**<br>that's why I've come |
| | (emphatic) | **pour moi, cet argument ne tient pas**<br>if you ask me, this argument isn't valid |

| | | |
|---|---|---|
| | (time) | **j'en ai pour une heure**<br>it'll take me an hour |
| | | **je suis en vacances pour 2 semaines**<br>I'm on holiday for 2 weeks |
| | *(**pour** stresses intention and future time: see **depuis**<br>and **pendant**, pp 214 and 218)* | |
| | (idiom) | **c'est bon pour la santé**<br>it's good for your health |
| *to* | (+ infinitive) | **il était trop paresseux pour<br>réussir ses examens**<br>he was too lazy to pass his exams |

## .près de.

| | | |
|---|---|---|
| *near* | (place) | **près du marché**<br>near the market |
| *nearly* | (time) | **il est près de minuit**<br>it's nearly midnight |
| | (quantity) | **près de cinquante**<br>nearly fifty |

## .quant à.

| | | |
|---|---|---|
| *as for* | | **quant à moi**<br>as for me |

## .sans.

| | | |
|---|---|---|
| *without* | (+ noun) | **sans espoir**<br>without hope |
| | (+ pronoun) | **je n'irai pas sans vous**<br>I won't go without you |
| | (+ infinitive) | **sans parler**<br>without speaking<br>**sans s'arrêter**<br>without stopping |

## .sauf.

*except for*      **ils sont tous partis, sauf John**
everyone left except John

*barring*      **sauf accidents/sauf imprévu**
barring accidents/the unexpected

## .selon.

*according to*      **selon le président**
according to the President
**selon moi**
in my opinion

## .sous.

*under*      (physical)      **sous la table**
under the table

(governed by)      **sous Élisabeth II**
under Elizabeth II

*in*      (weather)      **sous la pluie**
in the rain

(idiom)      **sous peu**
before long/shortly
**sous la main**
to hand
**sous tous rapports**
in all respects
**sous mes yeux**
before my eyes

## .sur.

*on/upon*      (place)      **le chat est sur le toit**
the cat's on the roof

*off*      **je l'ai pris sur l'étagère**
I took it off the shelf

| | | |
|---|---|---|
| *out of* | (proportion) | **neuf sur dix**<br>nine out of ten |
| | | **une semaine sur trois**<br>one week in three |
| *over* | (place) | **le pont sur la Loire**<br>the bridge over the Loire |
| | | **l'emporter sur quelqu'un**<br>to prevail over someone |
| *about* | (idiom) | **une enquête sur …**<br>an enquiry about … |
| *at* | | **sur ces paroles**<br>at these words |
| | | **sur ce, il est sorti**<br>at this he went out |
| *by* | | **quatre mètres sur cinq**<br>four metres by five |
| *in* | | **sur un ton amer**<br>in a bitter tone (of voice) |

### .vers.

| | | |
|---|---|---|
| *towards* | (place) | **vers le nord**<br>towards the north |
| | (time) | **vers la fin du match**<br>towards the end of the match |
| *about* | (time) | **vers 10 heures**<br>about 10 o'clock |

### .voici/voilà.

| | | |
|---|---|---|
| *here* | | **le voici qui vient**<br>here he comes |
| *there* | | **voilà où il demeure**<br>that's where he lives |

# 9. CONJUNCTIONS

Conjunctions are words or expressions which link words, phrases or clauses. They fall into two categories, coordinating conjunctions and subordinating conjunctions:

## A. Coordinating Conjunctions

### 1. Definition

These link two similar words or groups of words, eg nouns, pronouns, adjectives, adverbs, prepositions, phrases or clauses. The principal coordinating conjunctions (or adverbs used as conjunctions) are:

| | | |
|---|---|---|
| **et**<br>and | **mais**<br>but | **ou**<br>or |
| **ou bien**<br>or (else) | **soit**<br>either | **ni**<br>neither |
| **alors**<br>then | **aussi**<br>therefore | **donc**<br>then, therefore |
| **puis**<br>then *(next)* | **car**<br>for *(because)* | **or**<br>now |
| **cependant**<br>however | **néanmoins**<br>nevertheless | **pourtant**<br>yet, however |
| **toutefois**<br>however | | |

**il est malade mais il ne veut pas aller au lit**
he's ill but he won't go to bed

**il faisait beau alors il est allé se promener**
it was nice weather so he went for a walk

## 2. Repetition

**a)** Some coordinating conjunctions are repeated:

> **soit … soit …**                    either … or …
> **ou (bien) … ou (bien) …**          either … or …
>
> **prenez soit l'un soit l'autre**
> take one or the other
>
> **soit tu viens avec nous, soit tu restes ici mais tu te décides**
> either you come with us or you stay here, but you have to decide
>
> **ou tu t'habitues ou tu démissionnes**
> either you get used to it or you resign
>
> **ni … ni …**    neither … nor …
>
> **le vieillard n'avait ni amis ni argent**
> the old man had neither friends nor money

**b)** **et** and **ou** can be repeated in texts of a literary nature:

> **et … et …**    both … and …
>
> **ou … ou …**    either … or …
>
> **elle ne cessa et de crier et de pleurer**
> she didn't stop shouting and crying
>
> **ou c'est lui ou c'est moi !**
> it's either him or me!

## 3. aussi

**aussi** means 'therefore' only when placed before the verb. The subject pronoun is placed after the verb (see p 244).

> **il pleuvait, aussi Pascal n'est-il pas sorti**
> it was raining, so Pascal didn't go out

When **aussi** follows the verb it means 'also':

> **j'ai aussi emporté des pulls, au cas où**
> I also brought some jumpers, just in case

# B. Subordinating Conjunctions

These join a subordinate clause to another clause, usually a main clause.
The principal subordinating conjunctions are:

| | | | |
|---|---|---|---|
| comme | as | parce que | because |
| puisque | since | ainsi que | (just) as |
| à mesure que | as | tant que | as long as |
| avant que | before | après que | after |
| jusqu'à ce que | until | depuis que | since |
| pendant que | while | tandis que | whereas |
| si | if | à moins que | unless |
| pourvu que | provided that | quoique | although |
| bien que | although | quand | when |
| lorsque | when | dès que | as soon as |
| aussitôt que | as soon as | pour que | in order that |
| afin que | so that | de sorte que | so that |
| de façon que | so that | de peur que (+ ne) | for fear that, lest |

Note that some subordinating conjunctions require the subjunctive
(see pp 137-8).

## C. Que

### 1. Coordinating (see pp 48-9 and 59-61)

que is a coordinating conjunction when used in comparisons:

> **il est plus fort que moi**
> he is stronger than I

> **elle est plus courageuse que tu ne crois**
> she's braver than you think

### 2. Subordinating

**a)** *meaning 'that':*

> **elle dit qu'elle l'a vu**
> she says she has seen him

> **il faut que tu viennes**
> you'll have to come

> **je pense que tu as raison**
> I think you're right

> **il paraît qu'elle a gagné**
> it seems she's won

**b)** *replacing another conjunction:*

When a conjunction introduces more than one verb, **que** usually replaces the second subordinating conjunction and any subsequent ones to avoid repetition:

> **comme il était tard et que j'étais fatigué, je suis rentré**
> as it was late and I was tired, I went home

> **s'il fait beau et que tu es libre, nous irons à la piscine**
> if the weather's nice and you're free, we'll go to the swimming pool

> **nous sortirons lorsque nous aurons déjeuné et que tu te seras reposé**
> we'll go out when we've had lunch and you've had a rest

# 10. NUMBERS AND QUANTITY

## A. Cardinal Numbers

| | | | |
|---|---|---|---|
| 0 | zéro | 40 | quarante |
| 1 | un (une) | 50 | cinquante |
| 2 | deux | 60 | soixante |
| 3 | trois | 70 | soixante-dix |
| 4 | quatre | 71 | soixante et onze |
| 5 | cinq | 72 | soixante-douze |
| 6 | six | 80 | quatre-vingt(s) |
| 7 | sept | 90 | quatre-vingt-dix |
| 8 | huit | 99 | quatre-vingt-dix-neuf |
| 9 | neuf | 100 | cent |
| 10 | dix | 101 | cent un(e) |
| 11 | onze | 102 | cent deux |
| 12 | douze | 121 | cent vingt et un(e) |
| 13 | treize | 122 | cent vingt-deux |
| 14 | quatorze | 200 | deux cents |
| 15 | quinze | 201 | deux cent un(e) |
| 16 | seize | 1000 | mille |
| 17 | dix-sept | 1988 | mille neuf cent |
| 18 | dix-huit | | quatre-vingt-huit |
| 19 | dix-neuf | 2000 | deux mille |
| 20 | vingt | 10,000 | dix mille |
| 30 | trente | 1,000,000 | un million |

*Note:*

a) **un** is the only cardinal number which agrees with the noun in gender:

| | |
|---|---|
| un kilo | une pomme |
| a kilo | an apple |

b)  hyphens are used in compound numbers between 17 and 99 except where **et** is used (this also applies to compound numbers after 100: **cent vingt-trois** 123).

c)  **cent** and **mille** are not preceded by **un** as in English (one hundred).

d)  **vingt** and **cent** multiplied by a number take an **s** when they are not followed by another number.

>   **il a quatre-vingts ans**
>   he's eighty

>   **elle a remporté quatre-vingt-deux victoires**
>   she has notched up eighty-two wins

>   **c'est une civilisation vieille de huit cents ans**
>   it's a civilization which is eight hundred years old

>   **ce livre compte trois cent cinq pages**
>   ' this book has three hundred and five pages

e)  **mille** is invariable.

>   **trente mille personnes ont assisté à la rencontre**
>   thirty thousand people went to the match

## B. Ordinal Numbers

|  |  | abbreviation |
|---|---|---|
| 1st | premier/première | $1^{er}/1^{ère}$ |
| 2nd | deuxième/second | $2^e$ |
| 3rd | troisième | $3^e$ |
| 4th | quatrième | $4^e$ |
| 5th | cinquième | $5^e$ |
| 6th | sixième | $6^e$ |
| 7th | septième | $7^e$ |
| 8th | huitième | $8^e$ |
| 9th | neuvième | $9^e$ |
| 10th | dixième | $10^e$ |
| 11th | onzième | $11^e$ |
| 12th | douzième | $12^e$ |
| 13th | treizième | $13^e$ |
| 14th | quatorzième | $14^e$ |
| 15th | quinzième | $15^e$ |
| 16th | seizième | $16^e$ |
| 17th | dix-septième | $17^e$ |
| 18th | dix-huitième | $18^e$ |
| 19th | dix-neuvième | $19^e$ |
| 20th | vingtième | $20^e$ |
| 21st | vingt et unième | $21^e$ |
| 22nd | vingt-deuxième | $22^e$ |
| 30th | trentième | $30^e$ |
| 100th | centième | $100^e$ |
| 101st | cent unième | $101^e$ |
| 200th | deux centième | $200^e$ |
| 1000th | millième | $1000^e$ |
| 10,000th | dix millième | $10\ 000^e$ |

Note:

a) ordinal numbers are formed by adding **-ième** to cardinal numbers, except for **premier** and **second**; **cinq**, **neuf** and numbers ending in **e** undergo slight changes: **cinquième, neuvième, onzième, douzième** etc.

b) ordinal numbers agree with the noun in gender and number:

**le Premier ministre**
the Prime Minister

**la première fleur**
**du printemps**
the first flower of spring

c) there is no elision with **huitième** and **onzième**:

**le huitième jour**
the eighth day

**du onzième candidat**
of the eleventh candidate

d) cardinal numbers are used for monarchs, except for 'first':

**Charles deux**
Charles II

**Charles premier**
Charles I

## C. Fractions And Proportions

### 1. Fractions

Fractions are expressed as in English: cardinal followed by ordinal:

**deux cinquièmes**
two fifths

*But:*   $\frac{1}{4}$ **un quart**      $\frac{1}{2}$ **un demi, une demie**

   $\frac{1}{3}$ **un tiers**      $\frac{3}{4}$ **trois quarts**

### 2. Decimals

The English decimal point is conveyed by a comma in French:

**un virgule huit (1,8)**
one point eight (1.8)

### 3. Approximate numbers

| | |
|---|---|
| **une huitaine**<br>about eight | **une dizaine**<br>about ten |
| **une trentaine**<br>some thirty | **une centaine**<br>about a hundred |

*But:*   **un millier**
about a thousand

Note that **de** is used when the approximate number is followed by a noun:

**une vingtaine d'enfants**
about twenty children

### 4. Arithmetic

| | | |
|---|---|---|
| Addition: | deux plus quatre | 2+4 |
| Subtraction: | cinq moins deux | 5−2 |
| Multiplication: | trois fois cinq | 3×5 |
| Division: | six divisé par deux | 6÷2 |
| Square: | deux au carré | $2^2$ |
| Power: | deux puissance six | $2^6$ |

## D. Measurements And Prices

### 1. Measurements

a) *Dimensions*

| | |
|---|---|
| long(ue)/de longueur/de long | long |
| profond(e)/de profondeur/de profond | deep |
| épais(se)/d'épaisseur | thick |
| haut(e)/de hauteur/de haut | high |

**la salle de classe est longue de 12 mètres**
**la salle de classe a/fait 12 mètres de longueur/de long**
the classroom is 12 metres long

**ma chambre fait quatre mètres sur trois**
my bedroom is about four metres by three

b) *Distance*

**à quelle distance sommes-nous de la gare?**
how far are we from the station?

**nous sommes à deux kilomètres de la gare**
we are two kilometres from the station

**combien y a-t-il d'ici à Blois?**
how far is it to Blois?

### 2. Price

**ce pull m'a coûté 20 euros**
this sweater cost me 20 euros

**j'ai payé ce pull 20 euros**
I paid 20 euros for this sweater

**des pommes à 2 euros le kilo**
apples at 2 euros a kilo

**du vin blanc à 3 euros la bouteille**
white wine at 3 euros a bottle

**cela fait/revient à 6 euros**
that comes to 6 euros

**ils coûtent 4 euros pièce**
they cost 4 euros each

# E. Expressions Of Quantity

Quantity may be expressed by an adverb of quantity, eg 'a lot', 'too much' or by a noun which names the actual quantity involved, eg 'a bottle', 'a dozen'.

## 1. Expression of quantity + 'de' + noun

Before a noun, adverbs and other expressions of quantity are followed by **de** (**d'** before a vowel or a silent **h**) and never by **du, de la** or **des**, except for **bien des** and **la plupart du/des**:

| | |
|---|---|
| **assez de**<br>enough | **autant de**<br>as much/many |
| **beaucoup de**<br>a lot of/much/many | **combien de**<br>how much/many |
| **moins de**<br>less/fewer | **plus de**<br>more |
| **peu de**<br>little/few | **un peu de**<br>a little |
| **tant de**<br>so much/many | **tellement de**<br>so much/many |
| **bien du/de la/des**<br>many/a lot of | **la plupart du/de la/des**<br>most |
| **trop de**<br>too much/many | |

| | |
|---|---|
| **il y a assez de fromage?**<br>is there enough cheese? | **autant de gens**<br>as many people |
| **je n'ai pas beaucoup de temps**<br>I haven't got much time | **il y a combien de pièces?**<br>how many rooms are there? |
| **j'ai mis moins de temps que lui**<br>I took less time than him | **mange plus de légumes!**<br>eat more vegetables! |
| **peu de gens le savent**<br>not many people know that | **tu veux un peu de pain?**<br>would you like a little bread? |
| **il y a tant d'années**<br>so many years ago | **j'ai tellement de travail**<br>I've got so much work |

| | |
|---|---|
| **bien des gens**<br>a good many people | **la plupart des Français**<br>most French people |
| **tu as bien de la patience**<br>you have a lot of patience | **il y a trop de voitures**<br>there are too many cars |

## 2. Noun expressing quantity + 'de' + noun

| | |
|---|---|
| **une boîte de**<br>a box/tin/can/jar of | **une bouteille de**<br>a bottle of |
| **une bouchée de**<br>a mouthful of *(food)* | **une cuillerée de**<br>a spoonful of |
| **une douzaine de**<br>a dozen | **une gorgée de**<br>a mouthful of *(drink)* |
| **un kilo de**<br>a kilo of | **un litre de**<br>a litre of |
| **une livre de**<br>a pound of | **un morceau de**<br>a piece of |
| **un paquet de**<br>a packet of | **une paire de**<br>a pair of |
| **une part de**<br>a share/helping of | **une tasse de**<br>a cup of |
| **une tranche de**<br>a slice of | **un verre de**<br>a glass of |

**je voudrais une boîte de thon et un litre de lait**
I'd like a tin of tuna and a litre of milk

**il y a une boîte de limonade dans le frigo**
there's a can of lemonade in the fridge

**j'ai pris deux parts de choucroute**
I took two helpings of sauerkraut

**il a mangé une douzaine d'œufs et six morceaux de poulet**
he ate a dozen eggs and six pieces of chicken

## 3. Expressions of quantity used without a noun

When an expression of quantity is not followed by a noun, **de** is replaced by the pronoun **en** (see pp 82-4):

> **il y avait beaucoup de neige; il y en avait beaucoup**
> there was a lot of snow; there was a lot (of it)

> **elle a mangé trop de chocolats; elle en a trop mangé**
> she's eaten too many chocolates; she's eaten too many (of them)

# 11. EXPRESSIONS OF TIME

## A. The Time

**quelle heure est-il?**
what time is it?

**a)** *full hours*

**il est midi/minuit**
it is 12 noon *or* midday/midnight

**il est une heure**
it is 1 o'clock

**b)** *half-hours*

**il est minuit et demi(e)**
it is 12.30 a.m.

**il est midi et demi(e)**
it is 12.30 p.m.

**il est une heure et demie**
it is 1.30

**c)** *quarter-hours*

**il est deux heures un/et quart**
it is a quarter past two

**il est deux heures moins
le/un quart**
it is a quarter to two

**d)** *minutes*

**il est quatre heures vingt-trois**
it is 23 minutes past 4

**il est cinq heures moins
vingt**
it is 20 to 5

Note that **minutes** is usually omitted; **heures** is never omitted.

**e)** *a.m. and p.m.*

**du matin**
a.m., in the morning

**de l'après-midi/du soir**
p.m., in the evening

**il est sept heures moins dix
du matin**
it is 6.50 a.m. *or* in the morning

**il est sept heures dix du soir**
it is 7.10 p.m *or* in the evening

# EXPRESSIONS OF TIME

The 24-hour clock is commonly used:

**dix heures trente**　　　　　**quatorze heures trente-cinq**
10.30 a.m.　　　　　　　　　2.35 p.m.

**dix-neuf heures dix**
7.10 p.m.

Note that times are often abbreviated as follows:

**dix-neuf heures dix**　　　　19h10

## B. The Date

### 1. Names of months, days and seasons

a) *Months (les mois)*

| | |
|---|---|
| janvier | January |
| février | February |
| mars | March |
| avril | April |
| mai | May |
| juin | June |
| juillet | July |
| août | August |
| septembre | September |
| octobre | October |
| novembre | November |
| décembre | December |

b) *Days of the week (les jours de la semaine)*

| | |
|---|---|
| lundi | Monday |
| mardi | Tuesday |
| mercredi | Wednesday |
| jeudi | Thursday |
| vendredi | Friday |
| samedi | Saturday |
| dimanche | Sunday |

c) *Seasons (les saisons)*

| | |
|---|---|
| le printemps | spring |
| l'été | summer |
| l'automne | autumn |
| l'hiver | winter |

For prepositions used with the seasons see p 18.

Note that in French, months and days are masculine and do not have a capital letter unless they begin a sentence.

## 2. Dates

**a)** Cardinals (eg **deux, trois**) are used for the dates of the month except the first:

| | |
|---|---|
| **le quatorze juillet** | **le deux novembre** |
| the fourteenth of July | the second of November |

*But:* **le premier février**
the first of February

The definite article is used as in English; French does not use prepositions ('on' and 'of' in English):

**je vous ai écrit le trois mars**
I wrote to you on the third of March

**b)** **mil** (a thousand) is used instead of **mille** in dates from 1001 onwards:

**mil neuf cent quatre-vingt sept**
nineteen hundred and eighty-seven

**l'an deux mil deux**
the year two thousand and two

## 3. Année, journée, matinée, soirée

Année, journée, matinée, soirée (the feminine forms of **an, jour, matin** and **soir**) are usually found in the following cases:

**a)** *when duration is implied:*

| | |
|---|---|
| **pendant une année** | for a (whole) year |
| **toute la journée** | all day long, the whole day |
| **dans la matinée** | in the (course of the) morning |
| **passer une soirée** | to spend an evening |
| **l'année scolaire/universitaire** | the school/academic year |

**b)** *with an ordinal number or an indefinite expression:*

| | |
|---|---|
| **la deuxième année** | the second year |
| **dans sa vingtième année** | in his twentieth year |
| **plusieurs/quelques années** | several/a few years |
| **bien des/de nombreuses années** | many years |
| **environ une année** | about a year |

**c)** *with an adjective:*

| | |
|---|---|
| **de bonnes/mauvaises années** | good/bad years |

## C. Idiomatic Expressions

| | |
|---|---|
| à cinq heures | at five o'clock |
| à onze heures environ | (at) about eleven o'clock |
| vers minuit | (at) about midnight |
| vers (les) dix heures | (at) about ten o'clock |
| il est six heures passées | it's past six o'clock |
| à quatre heures précises/pile | at exactly four o'clock |
| sur le coup de trois heures | on the stroke of three |
| à partir de neuf heures | from nine o'clock onwards |
| peu avant sept heures | shortly before seven |
| peu après sept heures | shortly after seven |
| tôt ou tard | sooner or later |
| au plus tôt | at the earliest |
| au plus tard | at the latest |
| il est tard | it is late |
| il est en retard | he is late |
| il se lève tard | he gets up late |
| il est arrivé en retard | he arrived late |
| le train a vingt minutes de retard | the train is twenty minutes late |
| ma montre retarde de six minutes | my watch is six minutes slow |
| ma montre avance de six minutes | my watch is six minutes fast |
| ce soir | this evening, tonight |
| demain soir | tomorrow evening, tomorrow night |
| hier soir | yesterday evening, last night |
| samedi soir | Saturday evening |
| je sors samedi soir | I'm going out on Saturday night or evening |
| dans la soirée de samedi | on Saturday evening |
| dans la nuit de samedi (à dimanche) | during Saturday night |
| demain matin | tomorrow morning |
| hier matin | yesterday morning |
| lundi matin | Monday morning |

| | |
|---|---|
| j'y vais lundi matin | I'm going there on Monday morning |
| demain en huit | tomorrow week |
| le lendemain | the next day |
| le lendemain matin | the next morning |
| hier matin | yesterday morning |
| la semaine dernière | last week |
| la semaine prochaine | next week |
| la semaine qui vient | this coming week |
| je l'ai vu l'autre samedi | I saw him the other Saturday |
| lundi | on Monday |
| le lundi | on Mondays |
| je commence lundi | I'm starting (on) Monday |
| il vient le lundi | he comes on Mondays, he comes on a Monday |
| vient un lundi | come one Monday |
| un lundi sur deux | every other Monday, every second Monday |
| tous les lundis | every Monday |
| tous les lundis soirs | every Monday evening or night |
| tous mes lundis | all my Mondays |
| lundi en huit | a week on Monday, Monday week |
| lundi en quinze | a fortnight on Monday |
| il y a trois semaines | three weeks ago |
| il vient l'après-midi | he comes in the afternoon(s) |
| viens un après-midi | come one afternoon |
| une demi-heure | a half-hour, half an hour |
| un quart d'heure | a quarter of an hour |
| trois quarts d'heure | three quarters of an hour |
| passer son temps (à faire) | to spend one's time (doing) |
| perdre son temps | to waste one's time |
| de temps en temps | from time to time |
| de temps à autre | from time to time |
| dans les temps | on time |
| au début de l'après-midi/ de la soirée, en début de/ l'après-midi de soirée | in the early afternoon/ evening |

| | |
|---|---|
| je te téléphonerai au début de la matinée | I'll phone you first thing in the morning |
| au début du mois | at the beginning of the month |
| j'ai une réunion au milieu de la matinée *ou* en milieu de matinée | I have a meeting mid-morning |
| au milieu (du mois) de juin, (à la) mi-juin | in the middle of June, mid-June |
| au milieu de l'hiver | in the middle of winter, midwinter |
| j'ai une réunion à la fin de la matinée *ou* en fin de matinée | I have a meeting late morning |
| à la fin de l'hiver | at the end of the winter |
| on en reparlera fin janvier *ou* à la fin du mois de janvier | we'll talk about it again at the end of January |
| quel jour sommes-nous aujourd'hui? | what day is it today? |
| le combien sommes-nous aujourd'hui? | what's the date today?, what's today's date? |
| nous sommes/c'est le trois avril | it's the third of April |
| aujourd'hui nous sommes samedi | today is Saturday, it's Saturday today |
| vendredi 11 janvier 2002 | Friday, 11 January 2002 |
| nous nous sommes vus le vendredi 11 janvier | we saw each other on Friday, 11th January |
| le vendredi treize juillet | Friday the thirteenth of July |
| en février/au mois de février | in February/in the month of February |
| en février 2002 | in February 2002 |
| l'été 2002 | in the summer of 2002, in summer 2002 |
| en 2002 | in 2002 |
| dans les années soixante | in the sixties, in the 60s, in the 1960s |
| au début/à la fin des années soixante | in the early/late sixties |
| au dix-septième siècle | in the seventeenth century |
| au XVII$^e$ | in the 17th century |
| le jour de l'An | New Year's Day |

| | |
|---|---|
| **avoir treize ans** | to be thirteen (years old) |
| **être âgé de quatorze ans** | to be fourteen (years old) |
| **elle fête ses vingt ans** | she's celebrating her twentieth birthday |
| **elle a une vingtaine d'années** | she's around twenty (years old) |
| **un plan quinquennal** | a five-year plan |
| **une année bissextile** | a leap year |
| **une année civile** | a calendar year |
| **une année-lumière** | a light year |

# 12. THE SENTENCE

## A. Word Order

Word order is usually the same in French as in English, except in the following cases:

### 1. Adjectives

Many French adjectives follow the noun (see pp 45-7):

de l'argent *italien*
(some) *Italian* money

j'ai les yeux *bleus*
I've got *blue* eyes

### 2. Adverbs

In simple tenses, adverbs usually follow the verb (see p 58):

j'y vais *rarement*
I *seldom* go there

il fera *bientôt* nuit
it will *soon* be dark

### 3. Object pronouns

Object pronouns usually come before the verb (see pp 79-80):

je *t'*attendrai
I'll wait *for you*

il *la* lui a vendue
he sold *it* to him

### 4. Noun phrases

Noun phrases are formed differently in French (see pp 263-4):

une chemise en coton
a cotton shirt

le père de mon copain
my friend's father

### 5. Exclamations

The word order is not affected after **que** or **comme** (unlike after 'how' in English):

que tu es bête!
you *are* silly!
(how silly you are!)

qu'il fait froid!
it's so cold!

> comme il chante mal!
> he sings so badly!

> comme c'est beau!
> that's so beautiful!

## 6. DONT

**dont** must be followed by the subject of the clause it introduces; compare:

> l'ami dont j'ai perdu l'adresse
> the friend whose address I lost

> l'ami dont l'adresse a changé
> the friend whose address has changed

## 7. Inversion

In certain cases, the subject of a French clause is placed after the verb. Word order is effectively that of an interrogative sentence (see pp 249-50). This occurs:

**a)** *after the following, when they occur at the beginning of a clause:*

| à peine | aussi | peut-être |
|---------|-------|-----------|
| hardly  | therefore | maybe, perhaps |

> à peine Alain était-il sorti qu'il a commencé à pleuvoir
> Alain had barely gone out when it started raining

> il y avait une grève du métro, aussi a-t-il pris un taxi
> there was an underground strike, so he took a taxi

> peut-être vont-ils téléphoner plus tard
> maybe they'll phone later

*But:* Alain était à peine sorti qu'il a commencé à pleuvoir

ils vont peut-être téléphoner plus tard

**b)** *when a verb of saying follows direct speech:*

> 'si tu veux', a répondu Marie
> 'if you want', Marie replied

> 'attention!' a-t-elle crié
> 'watch out!', she shouted

> 'j'espère que non', dit-il
> 'I hope not', he said

> 'répondez!' ordonna-t-il
> 'answer!', he ordered

## B. Negative Expressions

### 1. Main negative words

a)

| | |
|---|---|
| ne ... pas | not |
| ne ... point | not (*literary*) |
| ne ... plus | no more/ longer, not ... any more |
| ne ... jamais | never |
| ne ... rien | nothing, not ... anything |
| ne ... guère | hardly |

b)

| | |
|---|---|
| ne ... personne | nobody, no one, not ... anyone |
| ne ... que | only |
| ne ... ni (ni ... ni) | neither ... nor |
| ne ... aucun(e) | no, not any, none |
| ne ... nul(le) | no |
| ne ... nulle part | nowhere, not ... anywhere |

*Note:*

i) **ne** becomes **n'** before a vowel or a silent **h**.

ii) **aucun** and **nul**, like other adjectives and pronouns, agree with the word they refer to; they are used only in the singular.

### 2. Position of negative expressions

a) *with simple tenses and with the imperative*

Negative words enclose the verb: **ne** comes before the verb, and the second part of the negative expression comes after the verb:

**je ne la connais pas**
I don't know her

**n'insistez pas!**
don't insist!

**je n'ai plus d'argent**
I haven't any money left

**tu ne le sauras jamais**
you'll never know

**ne dis rien**
don't say anything

**il n'y a personne**
no one's here

**je n'avais que 3 euros**
I only had 3 euros

**il n'est nulle part**
it isn't anywhere

tu n'as aucun sens de l'humour
you have no sense of humour

il n'est ni bête ni crédule
he's neither stupid nor gullible

**b)** *with compound tenses*

With **ne ... pas** and the other expressions in list **l a**, the word order is: **ne** + auxiliary + **pas** + past participle:

il n'est pas revenu
he didn't come back

je n'ai plus essayé
I didn't try any more

je n'avais jamais vu Paris
I had never seen Paris

on n'a rien fait
we haven't done anything

With **ne ... personne** and the other expressions in list **l b**, the word order is: **ne** + auxiliary + past participle + **personne/que/ni** etc:

il ne l'a dit à personne
he didn't tell anyone

tu n'en as acheté qu'un?
did you only buy one?

je n'en ai aimé aucun
I didn't like any of them

il n'est allé nulle part
he hasn't gone anywhere

**c)** *with the infinitive*

i) **ne ... pas** and the other expressions in list **l a** are placed together before the verb:

je préfère ne pas y aller
I'd rather not go

essaye de ne rien perdre
try not to lose anything

ii) **ne ... personne** and the other expressions in list **l b** enclose the infinitive:

il a été surpris de ne voir personne
he was surprised not to see anybody

j'ai décidé de n'en acheter aucun
I decided not to buy any of them

**d)** *at the beginning of a sentence*

When **personne**, **rien**, **aucun** and **ni ... ni ...** begin a sentence, they are followed by **ne**:

**personne ne le sait**
nobody knows

**rien n'a changé**
nothing has changed

**ni Paul ni Simone ne
sont venus**
neither Paul nor Simone came

**aucun secours n'est arrivé**
no help arrived

## 3. Combination of negative expressions

Negative expressions can be combined:

ne ... plus jamais
ne ... plus rien
ne ... plus personne
ne ... plus ni ... ni
ne ... plus que

ne ... jamais rien
ne ... jamais personne
ne ... jamais ni ... ni
ne ... jamais que

**on ne l'a plus jamais revu**
we never saw him again

**il n'y a plus rien**
there isn't anything left

**plus personne ne viendra**
no one will come any more

**tu ne dis jamais rien**
you never say anything

**je ne bois jamais que de l'eau**
I only ever drink water

**je ne vois jamais personne**
I never see anybody

**je ne pardonnerai jamais ni n'oublierai**
I will never forgive nor forget

## 4. Negative expressions without a verb

### a) PAS

**pas** (not) is the most common of all negatives; it is frequently used without a verb:

**tu l'aimes? – pas beaucoup**
do you like it? – not much

**ah non, pas lui!**
oh no, not him!

**non merci, pas pour moi**
no thanks, not for me

**un roman pas très long**
not a very long novel

**lui, il viendra, mais pas moi**
he will come, but I won't

**j'aime ça; pas toi?**
I like that; don't you?

## b) *NE*

**ne** is not used when there is no verb:

    **qui a crié? – personne**
    who shouted? – nobody

    **jamais de la vie!**
    not on your life!

    **rien! je ne veux rien!**
    nothing! I want nothing!

    **rien du tout**
    nothing at all

## c) *NON*

**non** (no) is always used without a verb:

    **tu aimes la natation? – non, pas du tout**
    do you like swimming? – no, not at all

    **tu viens, oui ou non? – je crois que non**
    are you coming, yes or no? – I don't think so

Note that **non plus** means 'neither':

    **je ne le crois pas – moi non plus**
    I don't believe him – neither do I

    **je n'ai rien mangé – nous non plus**
    I haven't eaten anything – neither have we

## C. Direct And Indirect Questions

### 1. Direct questions

There are three ways of forming direct questions in French:

**a)** *subject + verb (+ question word)*

The word order remains the same as in statements (subject + verb) but the intonation changes: the voice is raised at the end of the sentence. This is by far the most common question form in conversational French:

| | |
|---|---|
| **tu l'as acheté où?**<br>where did you buy it? | **je peux téléphoner d'ici?**<br>can I phone from here? |
| **vous prendrez quel train?**<br>which train will you take? | **tu me fais confiance?**<br>do you trust me? |
| **c'était comment?**<br>what was it like? | **la gare est près d'ici?**<br>is the station near here? |
| **le train part à quelle heure?**<br>what time does the train leave? | **cette robe me va?**<br>does this dress suit me? |

**b)** *(question word) + **est-ce que** + subject + verb*

This question form is also very common in conversation:

| | |
|---|---|
| **qu'est-ce que tu as?**<br>what's the matter with you? | **est-ce qu'il est là?**<br>is he in? |
| **est-ce que ton ami s'est amusé?**<br>did your friend have a good time? | |
| **où est-ce que vous avez mal?**<br>where does it hurt? | |

**c)** *inversion*

This question form is the most formal of the three, and the least commonly used in conversation:

i) If the subject is a pronoun, the word order is as follows:

(question word) + verb + hyphen + subject

| | |
|---|---|
| **où allez-vous?** | **voulez-vous commander?** |
| where are you going? | do you wish to order? |
| **quand est-il arrivé?** | **avez-vous bien dormi?** |
| when did he arrive? | did you sleep well? |

ii) If the subject is a noun, a pronoun referring to the noun is inserted after the verb, and linked to it with a hyphen:

(question word) + noun subject + verb + hyphen + pronoun

| | |
|---|---|
| **où ton père travaillait-il?** | **Nicole en veut-elle?** |
| where did your father work? | does Nicole want any? |

iii) **-t-** is inserted before **il** and **elle** when the verb ends in a vowel:

| | |
|---|---|
| **comment va-t-il voyager?** | **aime-t-elle le café?** |
| how will he travel? | does she like coffee? |
| **pourquoi a-t-il refusé?** | **Marie viendra-t-elle?** |
| why did he refuse? | will Marie be coming? |

Note that when a question word is used, modern French will often just invert the verb and the noun subject, without adding a pronoun; no hyphen is then necessary:

**où travaille ton père?**
where does your father work?

## 2. Indirect questions

**a)** *Definition*

Indirect questions follow a verb and are introduced by an interrogative word, eg:

ask him when he will arrive          I don't know why he did it

**b)** *Word order*

i) The word order is usually the same as in statements: question word + subject + verb:

| | |
|---|---|
| **je ne sais pas s'il voudra** | **dis-moi où tu l'as mis** |
| I don't know if he'll want to | tell me where you put it |

**il n'a pas dit quand il appellerait**
he didn't say when he would phone

ii) If the subject is a noun, the verb and subject are sometimes
inverted:

**demande-leur où est le camping**
ask them where the campsite is

*But:* **je ne comprends pas comment l'accident s'est produit**
I don't understand how the accident happened

**il ne savait pas pourquoi elle avait l'air triste**
he didn't know why she looked sad

## 3. Translation of English question tags

Examples of question tags are: isn't it? aren't you? doesn't he? won't
they? haven't you? is it? did you? and so on. Question tags are not
used in French as often as they are in English. Some of them can,
however, be translated in the following ways:

### i) n'est-ce pas?

**n'est-ce pas?** is used at the end of a sentence when confirmation of a
statement is expected:

**c'était très intéressant, n'est-ce pas?**
it was very interesting, wasn't it?

**tu voudrais partir en vacances, n'est-ce pas?**
you'd like to go on holiday, wouldn't you?

**vous n'arriverez pas trop tard, n'est-ce pas?**
you won't be arriving too late, will you?

### ii) hein? and non?

In conversation **hein?** and **non?** are often used after affirmative
statements instead of **n'est-ce pas**:

**il fait beau, hein?**
the weather's nice, isn't it?

**il est amusant, non?**
he's funny, isn't he?

# D. Answers ('Yes' And 'No')

## 1. OUI, SI and NON

a) **oui** and **si** mean 'yes' and are equivalent to longer affirmative answers such as 'yes, it is', 'yes, I will', 'yes, he has' etc:

> **tu m'écriras? – oui, bien sûr!**
> will you write to me? – (yes) of course I will

b) **non** means 'no' and is equivalent to longer negative answers such as 'no, it isn't', 'no, I didn't' etc:

> **c'était bien? – non, on s'est ennuyé**
> was it good? – no, it wasn't, we were bored

## 2. OUI or SI?

**oui** and **si** both mean 'yes', but **oui** is used to answer an affirmative question, and **si** to contradict a negative question:

> **cette place est libre? – oui**
> is this seat free? – yes (it is)

> **tu n'aimes pas lire? – si, bien sûr!**
> don't you like reading? – yes, of course (I do)

# 13. TRANSLATION PROBLEMS

## A. General Translation Problems

### 1. French words not translated in English

Some French words are not translated in English, particularly:

**a)** *Articles*

Definite and indefinite articles are not always translated (see pp 16-21):

> **dans** *la* **société moderne**
> in modern society

> *les* **gens en ont assez!**
> people have had enough!

> **ah non! encore** *du* **riz! je déteste** *le* **riz!**
> oh no! rice again! I hate rice!

**b)** *que*

**que** meaning 'that' as a conjunction (see p 225) or 'that'/'which'/
'whom' as a relative pronoun (see p 94) cannot be omitted in French:

> **j'espère** *que* **tu vas mieux**
> I hope you're better

> **elle pense** *que* **c'est vrai**
> she thinks it's true

> **celui** *que* **j'ai vu**
> the one I saw

> **c'est un pays** *que* **j'aime**
> it's a country I like

**c)** *Prepositions*

Some French verbs are followed by a preposition (+ indirect object)
when their English equivalent takes a direct object without a
preposition (see pp 204-5):

> **elle a téléphoné** *au* **médecin**
> she phoned the doctor

> **tu l'as dit** *à* **ton père?**
> did you tell your father?

### d) *le*

When **le** (it) is used in an impersonal sense (see p 79), it is not translated:

    **oui, je *le* sais**               **dis-*le*-lui**
    yes, I know                      tell him

## 2. English words not translated in French

Some English words are not translated in French, for example:

### a) *Prepositions*

i) with verbs which take an indirect object in English, but a direct object in French (see pp 203-4):

    **tu l'as payé combien?**        **écoutez cette chanson**
    how much did you pay *for* it?   listen *to* this song

ii) in certain expressions (see p 238):

    **je viendrai te voir lundi soir**
    I'll come and see you *on* Monday night

### b) *'can'*

'can' + verb of hearing or seeing (see p 165):

    **je ne vois rien!**             **tu entends la musique?**
    I can't see anything!        can you hear the music?

## 3. Other differences

### a) *English phrasal verbs*

Phrasal verbs are verbs which, when followed by a preposition, take on a different meaning, eg 'to give up', 'to walk out'. They do not exist in French and are translated by simple verbs or by expressions:

    to give up          to run away        to run across
    **abandonner**        **s'enfuir**          **traverser en courant**

### b) *English possessive adjectives*

English possessive adjectives (my, your etc) are translated by the

French definite article (**le/la/les**) when parts of the body are mentioned (see p 90):

| | |
|---|---|
| brush *your* teeth | he hurt *his* foot |
| **brosse-toi** *les* **dents** | **il s'est fait mal** *au* **pied** |

c) *'from'*

'from' is translated by **à** with verbs referring to taking something away (see p 206):

| | |
|---|---|
| he hid it *from* his parents | borrow some *from* your dad |
| **il l'a caché** *à* **ses parents** | **empruntes-en** *à* **ton père** |

# B. Specific Translation Problems

## 1. Words in -ing

The English verbal form ending in **-ing** is translated in a number of ways in French:

**a)** *by the appropriate French tense* (see p 126):

| | |
|---|---|
| he's speaking (present tense) | **il parle** |
| he was speaking (imperfect) | **il parlait** |
| he will be speaking (future) | **il parlera** |
| he has been speaking (perfect) | **il a parlé** |
| he had been speaking (pluperfect) | **il avait parlé** |
| he would be speaking (conditional) | **il parlerait** |

**b)** *by a French present participle* (see p 156)

i) as an adjective:

| | |
|---|---|
| **un livre amusant** | **c'est effrayant** |
| a funny book | it's frightening |

ii) as a verb, with **en** (while/on/by doing something; see pp 157-8):

**'ça ne fait rien', dit-il en souriant**
'it doesn't matter', he said smiling

**j'ai vu mes copains en sortant du lycée**
I saw my friends when I was coming out of school

Note, however, that **en** + present participle cannot be used when the two verbs have different subjects, eg:

I saw my brother coming out of school
**j'ai vu mon frère sortir du lycée/qui sortait du lycée**

**c)** *by a present infinitive* (see pp 146-54):

i) after a preposition:

| | |
|---|---|
| **au lieu de rire** | **avant de traverser** |
| instead of laughing | before crossing |

ii) after verbs of perception:

> **je l'ai entendu appeler**
> I heard him calling

> **je l'ai vue entrer**
> I saw her going in

iii) after verbs of liking and disliking:

> **j'adore faire du camping**
> I love camping

> **tu aimes lire?**
> do you like reading?

iv) after verbs followed by **à** or **de**:

> **tu passes tout ton temps à ne rien faire**
> you spend all your time doing nothing

> **il a commencé à neiger**
> it started snowing

> **continuez à travailler**
> go on working

> **tu as envie de sortir?**
> do you feel like going out?

> **il doit finir de manger**
> he must finish eating

v) when an English verb in **-ing** is the subject of another verb:

> **attendre serait inutile**
> waiting would be pointless

> **écrire est une corvée!**
> writing is a real chore!

vi) when an English verb in **-ing** follows 'is' or 'was' etc:

> **mon passe-temps favori, c'est de lire**
> my favourite pastime is reading

**d)** *by a perfect infinitive* (see p 154-5)

i) after **après** (after):

> **j'ai pris une douche après avoir nettoyé ma chambre**
> I had a shower after cleaning my room

ii) after certain verbs:

| | | |
|---|---|---|
| **regretter** | **remercier de** | **se souvenir de** |
| to regret | to thank for | to remember |

> **j'ai regretté de leur en avoir parlé**
> I regretted speaking to them about it

> **il m'a remercié d'être allé le chercher**
> he thanked me for going to pick him up

**e)** *by a noun*

particularly when referring to sports, activities, hobbies etc:

| | | |
|---|---|---|
| **le ski**<br>skiing | **la natation**<br>swimming | **l'équitation**<br>horse-riding |
| **la voile**<br>sailing | **le patinage**<br>skating | **le canoë**<br>canoeing |
| **la lecture**<br>reading | **la planche à voile**<br>windsurfing | **la cuisine**<br>cooking |
| **la boxe**<br>boxing | **la lutte**<br>wrestling | **la marche à pied**<br>walking |

## 2. IT IS (IT'S)

'it is' (it's) can be translated in three ways in French:

**a)** *il or elle* (see p 78)

**il** or **elle** are used with the verb **être** to translate 'it is', 'it was' etc (+ adjective) when referring to a particular masculine or feminine noun (a thing, a place etc):

> **merci de ta carte; elle était très amusante**
> thanks for your card; it was very funny

> **regarde ce blouson; il n'est vraiment pas cher**
> look at this jacket; it really isn't that expensive

**b)** *ce* (see pp 64-5)

**ce** (**c'** before a vowel) is used with the verb **être** to translate 'it is', 'it was' etc in two cases:

i) If **être** is followed by a word which is not an adjective on its own, ie by a noun, a pronoun, an expression of place etc:

> **c'était ta voix**
> it was your voice

> **c'est une grande maison**
> it's a big house

> **c'est moi! c'est Claude!**
> it's me! it's Claude!

> **c'est le tien?**
> is it yours?

**c'est en France que tu vas?**
is it France you're going to?

**c'est pour lundi**
it's for Monday

ii) If **être** is followed by an adjective which refers to something previously mentioned, such as an idea, an event or a fact, but not to a specific noun:

**l'homme n'ira jamais sur Saturne; ce n'est pas possible**
Man will never go to Saturn; it's not possible

**j'ai passé mes vacances en Italie; c'était formidable!**
I spent my holidays in Italy; it was great!

**oh, je m'excuse! – ce n'est pas grave**
oh, I'm sorry! – it's all right

c) *il* (see pp 122-5)

**il** is used to translate 'it is', 'it was' etc in three cases:

i) With **être** followed by an adjective + **de** or **que**, ie referring to something that follows, but not to a specific noun:

**il est impossible de connaître l'avenir**
it's impossible to know the future

**il est évident que tu ne me crois pas**
it's obvious you don't believe me

ii) To describe the weather (see p 122):

**il y a du vent**
it's windy

**il faisait très froid**
it was very cold

iii) With **être** to tell the time and in phrases relating to the time of day, or in such expressions as **il est temps de** (it's time to):

**il est deux heures du matin**
it's two in the morning

**il est tard!**
it's late!

**il est temps de partir**
it's time to go

Note that with other expressions of time, **c'est** is used:

**c'est lundi ou mardi aujourd'hui?**
is it Monday or Tuesday today?

**c'était l'été**
it was summer

## 3. TO BE

Although 'to be' is usually translated by **être**, it can also be translated in the following ways:

### a) *avoir*

i) **avoir** is used instead of **être** in many set expressions:

| | |
|---|---|
| avoir faim/soif | to be hungry/thirsty |
| avoir chaud/froid | to be warm/cold |
| avoir peur/honte | to be afraid/ashamed |
| avoir tort/raison | to be wrong/right |

ii) **avoir** is also used for age:

| | |
|---|---|
| quel âge as-tu? | j'ai vingt-cinq ans |
| how old are you? | I'm twenty-five |

### b) *aller*

**aller** is used for describing health:

| | |
|---|---|
| je vais mieux | tout le monde va bien |
| I am/feel better | everyone's fine |

### c) *faire*

**faire** is used in many expressions to describe the weather (see p 122):

| | |
|---|---|
| il fait beau | il fera chaud |
| the weather's nice | it will be hot |

Note that **il y a** can also be used to describe the weather, but only before **du/de la/des**:

**il y a du vent/des nuages/de la tempête**
it's windy/cloudy/stormy

### d) *untranslated*

'to be' is not translated when it is the first part of an English continuous tense; instead, the appropriate tense is used in French (see p 126):

| | |
|---|---|
| I'm having a bath | he was driving slowly |
| **je prends un bain** | **il conduisait lentement** |

## 4. ANY

'any' can be translated in three different ways:

**a)** *du/de la/des or de* (see pp 22-3)

The partitive article is used with a noun in negative and interrogative sentences:

| | |
|---|---|
| **il ne mange jamais de viande** | **tu veux du pain?** |
| he never eats meat | do you want any bread? |

**b)** *en* (see p 83)

**en** is used to translate 'any' when it occurs without a noun in negative and interrogative sentences:

| | |
|---|---|
| **je n'en ai pas** | **il en reste?** |
| I haven't got any | is there any left? |

**c)** *n'importe quel(le)/quel(le)s or tout(e)/tou(te)s*

these are used to translate 'any' (and 'every') when they mean 'no matter which':

**il pourrait arriver à n'importe quel moment**
he could arrive any time

**prends n'importe quelle couleur, je les aime toutes**
take any colour, I like them all

## 5. ANYONE, ANYTHING, ANYWHERE

Like 'any', these can be translated in different ways:

**a)** *in interrogative sentences:*

| | |
|---|---|
| **il y a quelqu'un?** | **tu l'as vu quelque part?** |
| is anyone in? | did you see it anywhere? |
| **il a dit quelque chose?** | |
| did he say anything? | |

**b)** *in negative sentences:*

| | |
|---|---|
| **il n'y a personne** | **je ne le vois nulle part** |
| there isn't anyone | I can't see it anywhere |

**je n'ai rien fait**
I didn't do anything

c) *in the sense of 'any' (and 'every'), 'no matter which':*

**n'importe qui peut le faire**
anyone can do that

**il croit n'importe quoi**
he believes anything

**j'irai n'importe où**
I'll go anywhere

**n'importe quand**
anytime

## 6. YOU, YOUR, YOURS, YOURSELF

French has two separate sets of words to translate 'you', 'your', 'yours', 'yourself':

a) tu, te (t'), toi, ton/ta/tes, le tien etc
b) vous, votre/vos, le vôtre etc

For their respective meanings and uses, see pp 77-8, 85-6, 89-90, 91-2.

a) *tu etc*

**tu, te, ton** etc correspond to the **tu** form of the verb (second person singular) and are used when speaking to one person you know well (a friend, a relative) or to someone younger. They represent the familiar form of address:

si *tu* viens au concert avec *ton* copain, je *t'*achète
deux places; une pour *toi* et une pour lui
if *you*'re coming to the concert with *your* boyfriend,
I'll get *you* two tickets; one for *you* and one for him

b) *vous etc*

**vous, vos** etc correspond to the **vous** form of the verb (second person plural) and are used:

i) when speaking to more than one person:

dépêchez-*vous*, les gars! *Vous* allez manquer le train
hurry up, boys! *You*'ll miss the train

ii) when speaking to one person you do not know well or to someone older. They represent the formal or polite form of address:

> **je regrette, Monsieur, mais *vous* ne pouvez pas garder *votre* chien avec *vous* dans ce restaurant**
> I'm sorry, sir, but *you* can't keep *your* dog with *you* in this restaurant

c) when speaking or writing to one person, you must not mix words from both sets, but decide whether you are being formal or familiar, and use the same form of address throughout:

> **Cher Michel,**
> **Merci de ta lettre. Comment vas-*tu*? ...**
> Dear Michel,
> Thanks for *your* letter. How are *you*? ...

> **Monsieur,**
> **Pourriez-*vous* me réserver une chambre dans *votre* hôtel pour le 8 juin?**
> Dear Sir,
> Could *you* book a room for me in *your* hotel for 8th June?

**vous** etc and **tu** etc can only be used together when **vous** is plural (ie when it refers to more than one person):

> *tu* sais, Jean, *toi* et *ta* sœur, *vous vous* ressemblez
> *you* know, Jean, *you* and *your* sister look like *each other*

## 7. Noun phrases

A noun phrase is a combination of two nouns used together to name things or people. In English, the first of these nouns is used to describe the second one, eg 'a love story'. In French, however, the position of the two nouns is reversed, so that the describing noun comes second and is linked to the first one by the preposition **de** (or **d'**):

| | |
|---|---|
| **une histoire d'amour**<br>a love story | **une feuille d'impôts**<br>a tax form |
| **un magasin de disques**<br>a record shop | **un acteur de cinéma**<br>a film actor |
| **un arrêt d'autobus**<br>a bus stop | **un film d'aventure**<br>an adventure film |

un coup de soleil
sunstroke

une boule de neige
a snowball

un roman de science-fiction
a science-fiction novel

un match de football
a football match

le château d'Édimbourg
Edinburgh castle

un conte de fées
a fairy tale

un joueur de rugby
a rugby player

un employé de bureau
an office worker

Note that when the describing noun refers to a type of material, the preposition **en** is often used instead of **de**:

un pull en laine
a woollen jumper

un pantalon en cuir
leather trousers

une bague en or
a gold ring

un sac en plastique
a plastic bag

## 8. Possession

In English, possession is often expressed by using a noun phrase and tagging **'s** at the end of the first word, eg:

my friend's cat

This is translated in French by: object + **de** + possessor:

le chat de mon ami

Note the use of the article **le/la/les**.

le fiancé de ma sœur
my sister's fiancé

les amis de Claire
Claire's friends

les événements de la semaine dernière
last week's events

When **'s** is used to refer to someone's house or shop etc, it is translated by the preposition **chez**:

je téléphone de chez Paul
I'm telephoning from Paul's (house)

chez le dentiste
at/to the dentist's

# INDEX

# INDEX

# INDEX

# INDEX